Mandolin
Songbook for Beginners

45 Oldies and Goldies American Songs with Tabs and Chords

 ONLINE
MP3

Collected and arranged by
Peter Upclaire

Peter Upclaire
Mandolin Songbook for Beginners
45 Oldies and Goldies American Songs with
Tabs and Chords

First edition: August 2021

Available from Amazon.com and other book
stores.

More information can be found online at
www.lovelymelodies.com.

Online MP3

Contents

Introduction

Young people often do not know the price of browsing the Internet. And my daughter also believes in the saying that you can get everything on the Internet for free. When she wanted to learn to play a few songs on guitar, she spent almost 1 hour searching for a single, not-too-quality song. When I told her that she would spend 100 hours of her life searching for 100 songs or, in other words, that she could earn $ 1,000 in 100 hours or play 100 hours more guitar, she began to think. But when I wanted to buy her a quality book of guitar songs, I couldn't find it. So I published my first paper and e-book in the field of music. Others followed, and this book is one of many.

The "Mandolin Songbook for Beginners" contains 45 of the most popular American old songs, which have delighted music lovers for several generations. As the title suggests, the book is intended primarily for beginners, but with the remark that the book is not intended for complete beginners. It is intended for those of you who, to some extent, already master the basics of music. I expect you to know what a tablature is, know three or more chords, and that you know how to rhythmically strum the strings.

Unlike other books, each song is presented with a melody in standard notation and tablature, with chord diagrams and lyrics. Thus, it can be used by almost complete beginners, as well as already musically educated musicians.

You can download free online audio tracks for all 45 songs at www.lovelymelodies.com. MP3s collected there are intended primarily for learning about traditional melodies. Since traditional melodies and lyrics change throughout history, we rarely find two identical melodies and lyrics of the same song in a certain period. Therefore, the songs in this book sometimes differ from the songs found on Youtube channels, and whose performances and arrangements are often copyrighted.

Due to the reduced cost of recording many songs from these books, the songs are recorded using computer programs and MIDI files arranged and used to print the book. Therefore, the performance of the song is somewhat mechanical, with no personal interpretations of the melody. And in some cases, the songs also lack the real sound of the instrument. Nevertheless, I found it better to add such music recordings to the book. A book with music recordings has a much greater value than a book without a piece of music. There are quite a few reasons for this. Listening to a song specifies the version of the melody. The song can be used to play while listening, and mechanical playing can also be used instead of the metronome. This will allow you to improve your playing technique. So your first task is to capture the given rhythm as accurately as possible.

The chords accompanying the melody are played at the beginning of each musical measure or when changing chords. Once you've mastered changing chords, you can find the right strumming pattern, as you've probably learned from books for complete beginners. In the beginning, it's best to play the chords next to each syllable of the song. And only a little later, try to find a suitable pattern that matches the whole melody of the song.

The book is also adapted for playing in a duet. The first instrument can play a melody and the second chords. Of course, you can also spice things up by singing.

But that's not all. All the songs from the books in this series are also adapted for other instruments. The song that someone plays on the mandolin is the same as in other books arranged for guitalele, ukulele, guitar, banjo, etc. Readers of books from this series who play different instruments can therefore play together at any time without any problems.

I arranged the songs so that playing requires as little effort as possible on the musician's part. I used the chords with open strings that produce the so-called ringing tones. These once extremely popular chords are intended for beginners and lovers of old sounds. For other contemporary-oriented musicians, I also added slightly more complex chords. I avoided the popular bare chords. These chords are difficult to play well, and the tones are often quite muted and shorter in duration.

Beginner Mandolin Chords

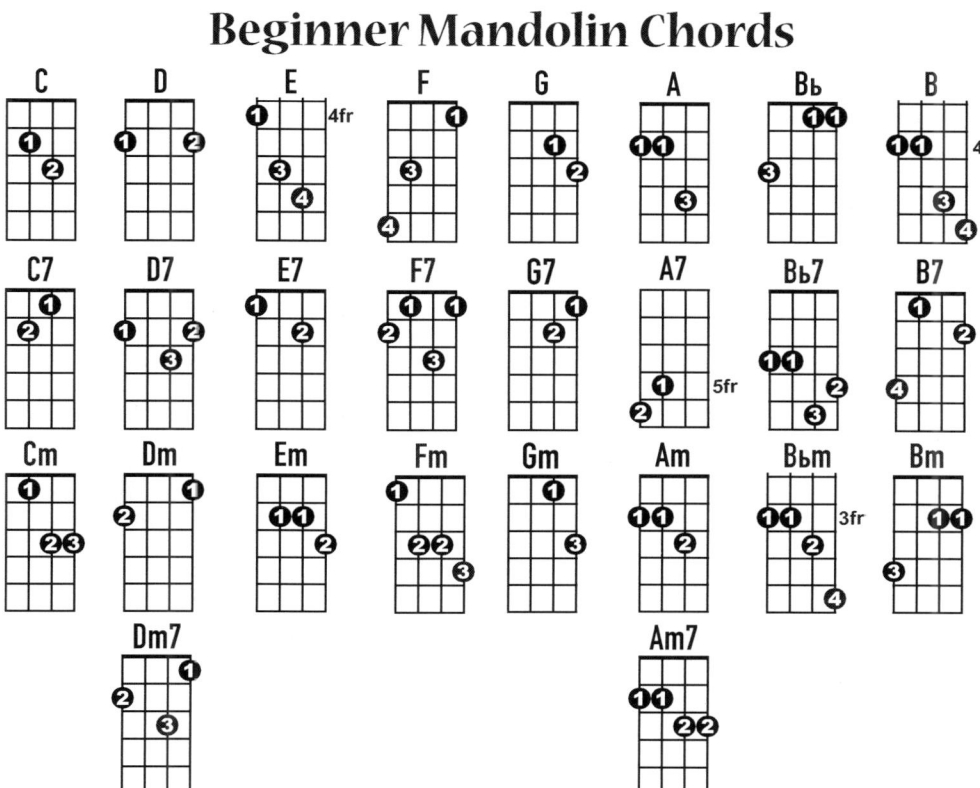

Intermediate Mandolin Chords

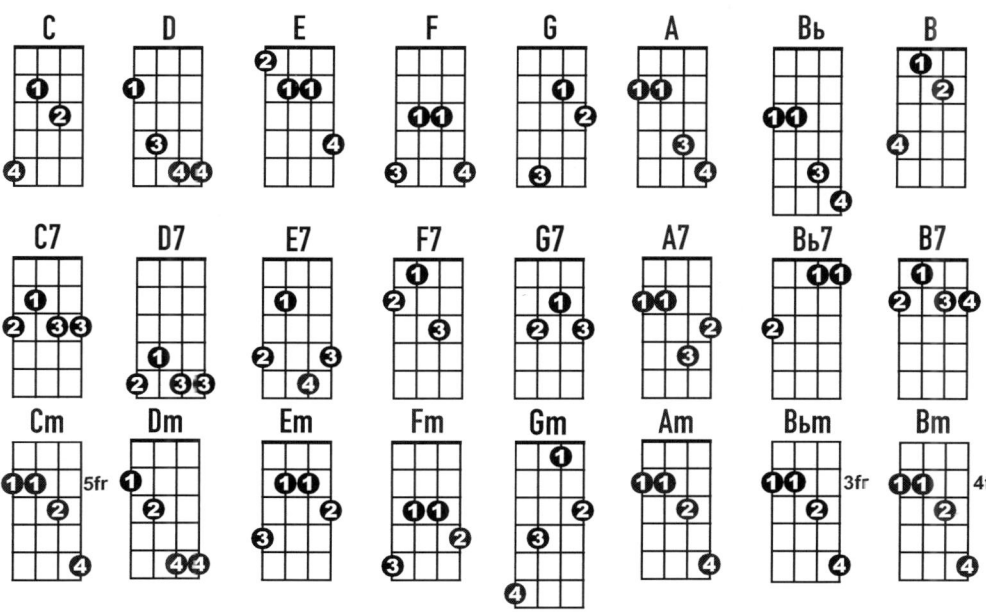

Amazing Grace

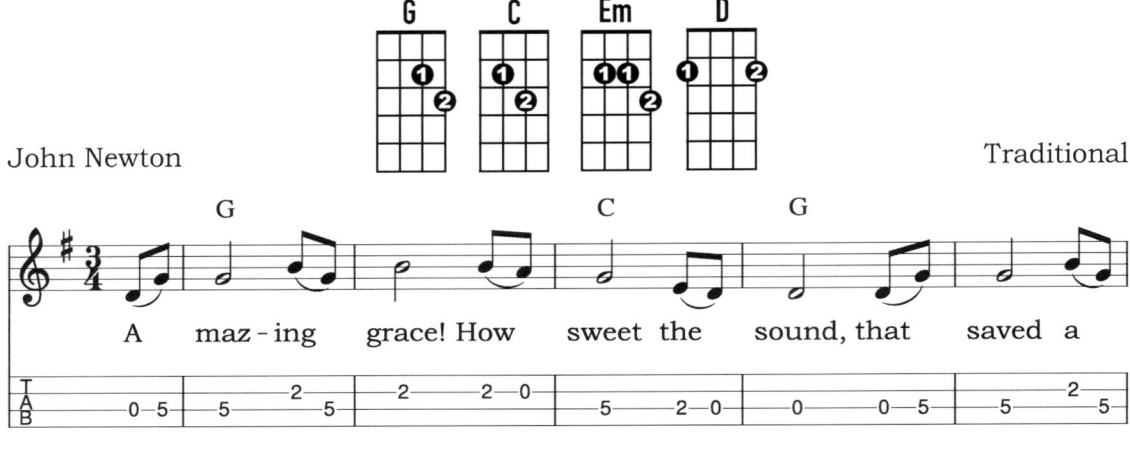

John Newton

Traditional

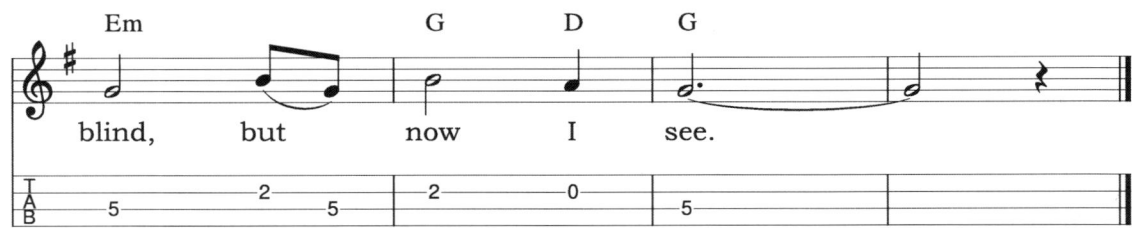

Amazing grace! How sweet the sound
That saved a wretch like me!
I once was lost, but now am found;
Was blind, but now I see.

Twas grace that taught my heart to fear,
And grace my fears relieved;
How precious did that grace appear
The hour I first believed.

Through many dangers, toils, and snares,
I have already come;
Tis grace hath brought me safe thus far,
And grace will lead me home.

The Lord has promised good to me,
His Word my hope secures;
He will my Shield and Portion be,
As long as life endures.

Yea, when this flesh and heart shall fail,
And mortal life shall cease,
I shall possess, within the veil,
A life of joy and peace.

The earth shall soon dissolve like snow,
The sun forbear to shine;
But God, who called me here below,
Will be forever mine.

When we've been there ten thousand years,
Bright shining as the sun,
We've no less days to sing God's praise
Than when we'd first begun.

Angelina Baker

Stephen C. Foster

left me here to weep a tear and beat on de old jaw - bone.

Way down on de old plantation dah's where I was born,
I used to beat de whole creation hoein in de corn;
Oh! den I work and den I sing so happy all de day,
Till Angelina Baker came and stole my heart away.

Chorus:
Angelina Baker! Angelina Baker's gone
She left me here to weep a tear
And beat on de old jawbone.

I've seen my Angelina in de spring-time and de fall,
I've seen her in de corn-field and I've seen her at de ball;
And ebry time I met her she was smiling like de sun,
But now I'm left to weep a tear cayse Angelina's gone.

Chorus

Angelina am so tall she nebber sees de ground,
She hab to take a wellumscope to look down on de town
Angelina likes de boys as far as she can see dem,
She used to run old Massa round to ax him for to free dem.

Chorus

Early in de morning ob a lubly summer day
I ax for Angelina, and dey say "she's gone away"
I don't know wha to find her, cayse I don't know wha she's gone,
She left me here to weep a tear and beat on de old jawbone.

Chorus

9

Aura Lea

Traditional

When the black-bird in the spring, on the wil-low tree,

sat and rocked, I heard him sing, sing-ing Au - ra Lea.

Au - ra Lea, Au - ra Lea, maid with gold - en hair.

Sun-shine came a - long with thee, and swal-lows in the air.

10

When the blackbird in the Spring,
On the willow tree,
Sat and rocked, I heard him sing,
Singing Aura Lea.
Aura Lea, Aura Lea,
Maid with golden hair;
Sunshine came along with thee,
And swallows in the air.

Aura Lea, Aura Lea,
Maid with golden hair;
Sunshine came along with thee,
And swallows in the air.

In thy blush the rose was born,
Music, when you spake,
Through thine azure eye the morn,
Sparkling seemed to break.
Aura Lea, Aura Lea,
Birds of crimson wing,
Never song have sung to me,
As in that sweet spring.

Aura Lea, Aura Lea,
Maid with golden hair;
Sunshine came along with thee,
And swallows in the air.

Aura Lea! the bird may flee,
The willow's golden hair
Swing through winter fitfully,
On the stormy air.
Yet if thy blue eyes I see,
Gloom will soon depart;
For to me, sweet Aura Lea
Is sunshine through the heart.

Aura Lea, Aura Lea,
Maid with golden hair;
Sunshine came along with thee,
And swallows in the air.

When the mistletoe was green,
Midst the winter's snows,
Sunshine in thy face was seen,
Kissing lips of rose.
Aura Lea, Aura Lea,
Take my golden ring;
Love and light return with thee,
And swallows with the spring.

Aura Lea, Aura Lea,
Maid with golden hair;
Sunshine came along with thee,
And swallows in the air.

11

Banks of Ohio

Traditional

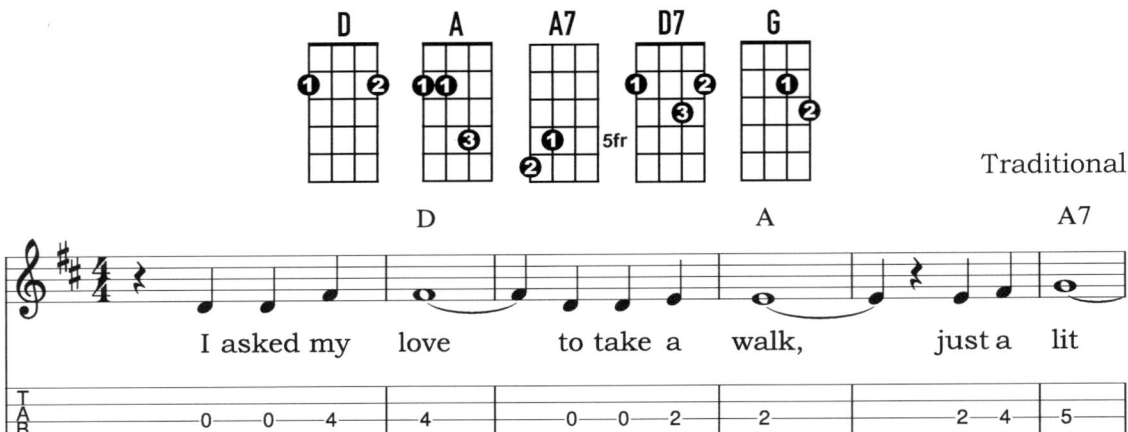

12

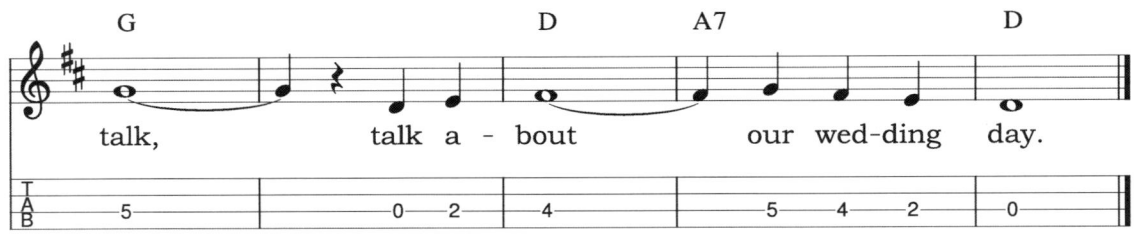

I asked my love to take a walk,
Just a little ways away.
While we walk along, we'll talk,
Talk about our wedding day.

Only say that you'll be mine,
And in our home we'll happy be.
Down beside where the waters flow,
Down by the banks of the Ohio.

I drew a knife against her throat,
As to my breasts she gently pressed.
"Oh, please, oh, please, don't murder me,
For I'm unprepared to die you see."

I've taken her by her lily-white hand,
I led her down and I7ve made her stand.
Then I plunged her to drown,
And I watched her as she floated down.

Returning home between twelve and one
Thinking of the deed I done."
I've murdered the girl I love you see,
Because she would not marry me.

That day I was returning home,
I met the sheriff, he came in the door.
He said: "Young men, come with me an go,
Down on the banks of the Ohio."

Billy Boy

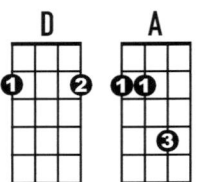

Traditional

Oh, where have you been, Bil-ly Boy, Bil-ly Boy, Oh,

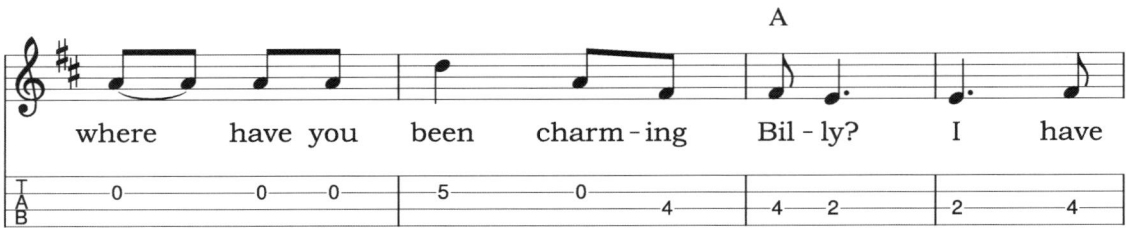

where have you been charm-ing Bil-ly? I have

14

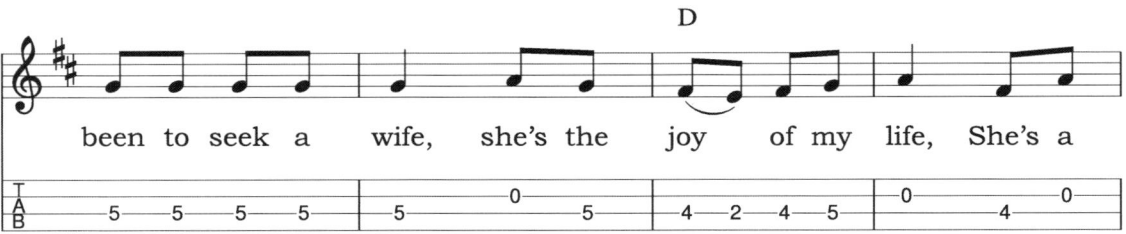

been to seek a wife, she's the joy of my life, She's a

young thing and can-not leave her mo-ther.

Oh, where have you been, Billy Boy, Billy Boy,
Oh, where have you been charming Billy?
I have been to seek a wife, she's the joy of my life,
She's a young thing and cannot leave her mother.

Did she ask you to come in, Billy Boy, Billy Boy,
Did she ask you to come in, charming Billy?
Yes, she asked me to come in, there's a dimple in her chin,
She's a young thing and cannot leave her mother.

Can she make a cherry pie, Billy Boy, Billy Boy,
Can she make a cherry pie, charming Billy?
She can make a cherry pie, quick as you can wink an eye,
She's a young thing and cannot leave her mother.

Can she make a feather bed, Billy Boy, Billy Boy,
Can she make a feather bed, charming Billy?
She can make a feather bed, while a-standing on her head,
She's a young thing and cannot leave her mother.

How tall is she, Billy Boy, Billy Boy,
How tall is she, charming Billy?
She is tall as any pine, and straight as a pumpkin vine,
She's a young thing and cannot leave her mother.

How old is she, Billy Boy, Billy Boy,
How old is she, charming Billy?
She is sixty times eleven, twenty-eight and forty- seven,
She's a young thing and cannot leave her mother!

Buffalo Gals

As I was walking down the street,
down the street, down the street,
a pretty girl I chanced to meet,
and she was pretty to see.

Buffalo gals won't you come out tonight,
Come out tonight, come out tonight.
Buffalo gals won't you come out tonight,
And dance by the light of the moon.

I asked her would she have some talk,
Have some talk, have some talk.
Her feet covered the whole sidewalk
As she stood close by me.

Buffalo gals won't you come out tonight,
Come out tonight, come out tonight.
Buffalo gals won't you come out tonight,
And dance by the light of the moon.

I asked her would she have a dance,
Have a dance, have a dance.
I thought I might get a chance
To shake a foot with her.

Buffalo gals won't you come out tonight,
Come out tonight, come out tonight.
Buffalo gals won't you come out tonight,
And dance by the light of the moon.

I'd like to make that gal my wife,
Gal my wife, gal my wife.
I'd be happy all my life.
If I had her by me.

Buffalo gals won't you come out tonight,
Come out tonight, come out tonight.
Buffalo gals won't you come out tonight,
And dance by the light of the moon.

Bury Me Not on the Lone Prairie

Traditional

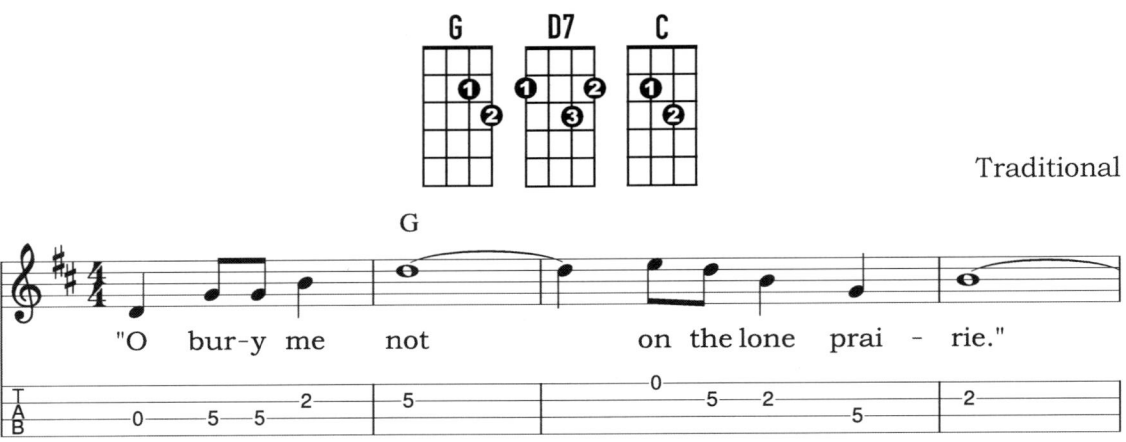

"O bur-y me not   on the lone prai - rie."

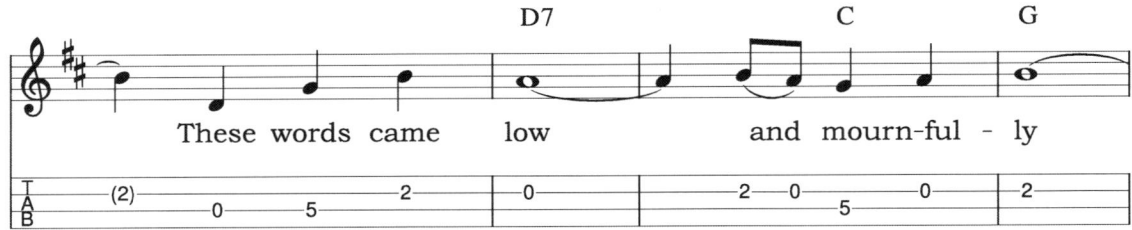

These words came   low   and mourn-ful - ly

18

From the pal-lid   lips   of the youth who   lay

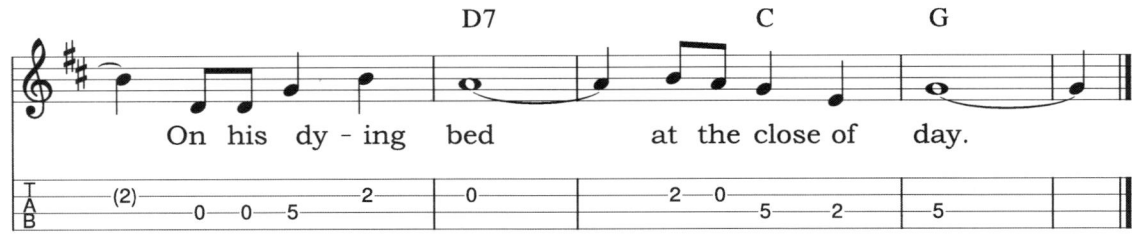

On his dy - ing bed   at the close of   day.

"O bury me not on the lone prairie."
These words came low and mournfully
From the pallid lips of the youth who lay
On his dying bed at the close of day.

He had wasted and pined 'til o'er his brow
Death's shades were slowly gathering now
He thought of home and loved ones nigh,
As the cowboys gathered to see him die.

"O bury me not on the lone prairie
Where coyotes howl and the wind blows free
In a narrow grave just six by three—
O bury me not on the lone prairie"

"It matters not, I've been told,
Where the body lies when the heart grows cold
Yet grant, o grant, this wish to me
O bury me not on the lone prairie."

"I've always wished to be laid when I died
In a little churchyard on the green hillside
By my father's grave, there let me be,
O bury me not on the lone prairie."

"I wish to lie where a mother's prayer
And a sister's tear will mingle there.
Where friends can come and weep o'er me.
O bury me not on the lone prairie."

"For there's another whose tears will shed.
For the one who lies in a prairie bed.
It breaks me heart to think of her now,
She has curled these locks, she has kissed this brow."

"O bury me not..." And his voice failed there.
But they took no heed to his dying prayer.
In a narrow grave, just six by three
They buried him there on the lone prairie.

And the cowboys now as they roam the plain,
For they marked the spot where his bones were lain,
Fling a handful o' roses o'er his grave
With a prayer to God his soul to save.

Camptown Races

Stephan. C. Foster

20

bob - tail   nag,   Some - bod - y   bet   on   de   bay.

Camptown ladies sing dis song, Doo-dah! doo-dah!
Camptown race-track five miles long, Oh, doo-dah day!
I come down dah wid my hat caved in, Doo-dah! doo-dah!
I go back home wid a pocketful of tin, Oh, doo-dah day!

Chorus:
Gwine to run all night!
Gwine to run all day!
I'll bet my money on de bob-tail nag,
Somebody bet on de bay.

De long tail filly and de big black hoss, Doo-dah! doo-dah!
Dey fly de track and dey both cut across, Oh, doo-dah day!
De blind hoss sticken in a big mud hole, Doo-dah! doo-dah!
Can't touch bottom wid a ten foot pole, Oh, doo-dah day!

Gwine to run all night!
Gwine to run all day!
I'll bet my money on de bob-tail nag,
Somebody bet on de bay.

Old muley cow come on to de track. Doo-dah! doo-dah!
De bob-tail fling her ober his back. Oh! doo-dah-day!
Den fly along like a rail-road car. Doo-dah! doo-dah!
Runnin "a race wid a shootin" star. Oh! doo-dah-day!

Gwine to run all night!
Gwine to run all day!
I'll bet my money on de bob-tail nag,
Somebody bet on de bay.

See dem flyin' on a ten mile heat, Doo-dah! doo-dah!
Round de race track, den repeat, Oh, doo-dah day!
I win mv money on de bob-tail nag, Doo-dah! doo-dah!
I keep my money in an old tow- bag, Oh, doo-dah day!

Gwine to run all night!
Gwine to run all day!
I'll bet my money on de bob-tail nag,
Somebody bet on de bay.

21

Cindy, Cindy

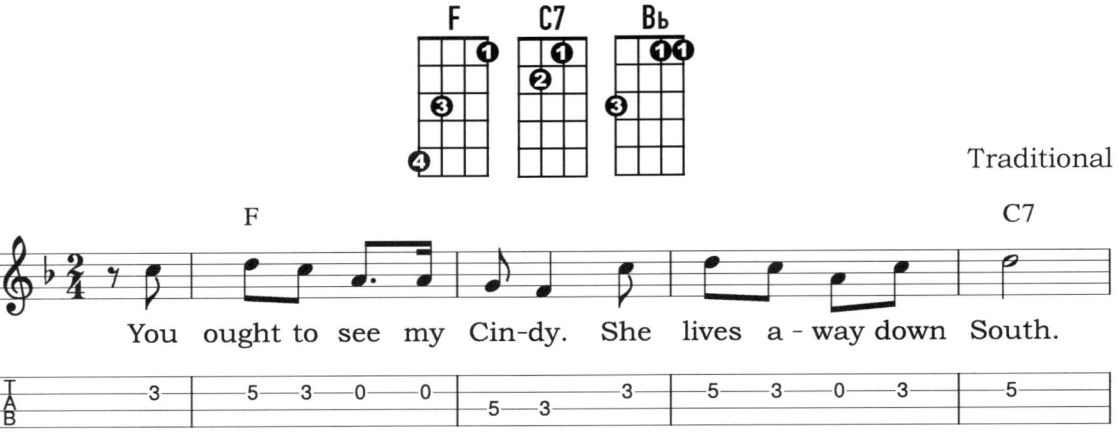

Traditional

22

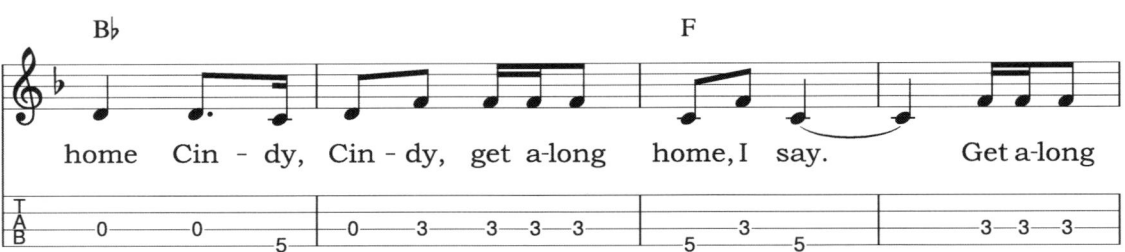

You ought to see my Cindy
She lives away down South.
She's so sweet the honey bees,
Swarm around her mouth.

Chorus:
Get along home Cindy, Cindy
Get along home, I say.
Get along home Cindy, Cindy
I'll marry you some day.

The first time that I saw her
She was standing in the door,
Her shoes and stockings in her hand
Her little bare feet on the floor.

Chorus

Well Cindy got religion
She had it once before,
But when she heard my old banjo,
She's the first one on the floor.

Chorus

I wish I was an apple
Hanging on a tree,
And every time my Cindy'd pass
She'd take a bite of me.

23

Chorus

I wish I had a needle and thread
As fine as I could sew,
I'd sew that girl right to my side
And down the road we'd go.

Chorus

Cindy hugged and kissed me
She wrung her hands and cried,
I swear she was the prettiest thing
That ever lived or died.

Chorus

Cindy in the summertime
Cindy in the fall,
If I can't have Cindy all the time
I'll have no one at all.

Down in the Valley

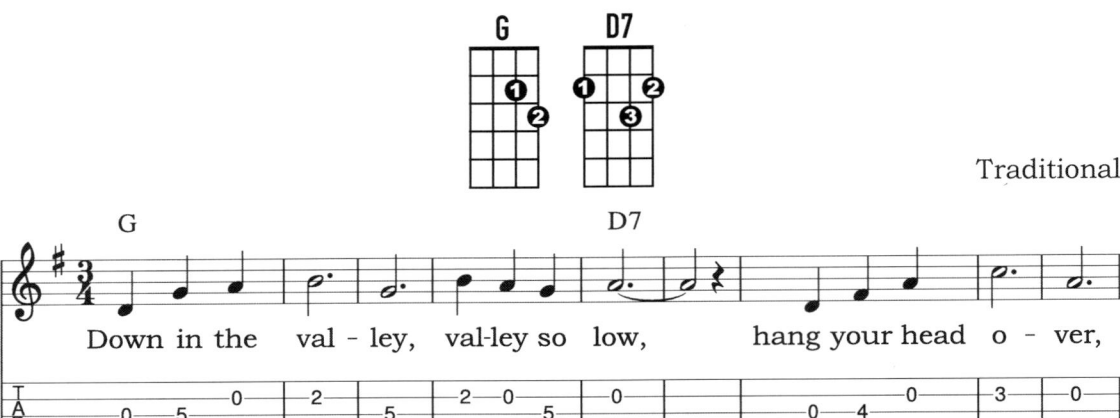

Traditional

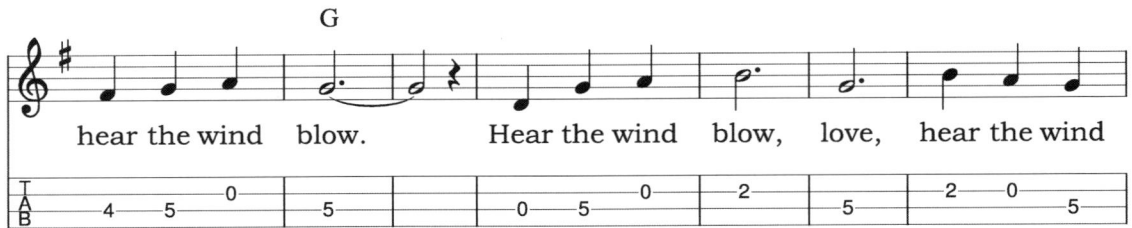

24

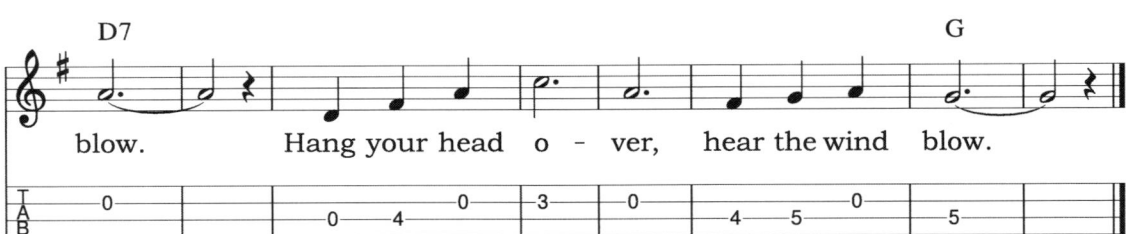

Down in the valley, valley so low.
Hang your head over hear the wind blow.
Hear the wind blow, dear, hear the wind blow.
Hang your head over hear the wind blow.

Roses love sunshine; violets love dew.
Angels in heaven know I love you.
Know I love you dear, know I love you.
Angels in heaven know I love you.

If you don't love me, love, whom you please.
Throw your arms 'round me, give my heart ease.
Give my heart ease, love, give my heart ease.
Throw your arms round me, give my heart ease.

Build me a castle forty feet high
So I can see him as he rides by.
As he rides by, love, as he rides by.
So I can see him as he rides by.

Write me a letter, send it by mail.
Send it in care of Birmingham jail.
Birmingham jail, love, Birmingham jail.
Send it in care of Birmingham jail.

Down in the valley, valley so low.
Hang your head over, hear the wind blow.
Hear the wind blow, love, hear the wind blow.
Hang your head over, hear the wind blow.

Get Along Littie Dogies

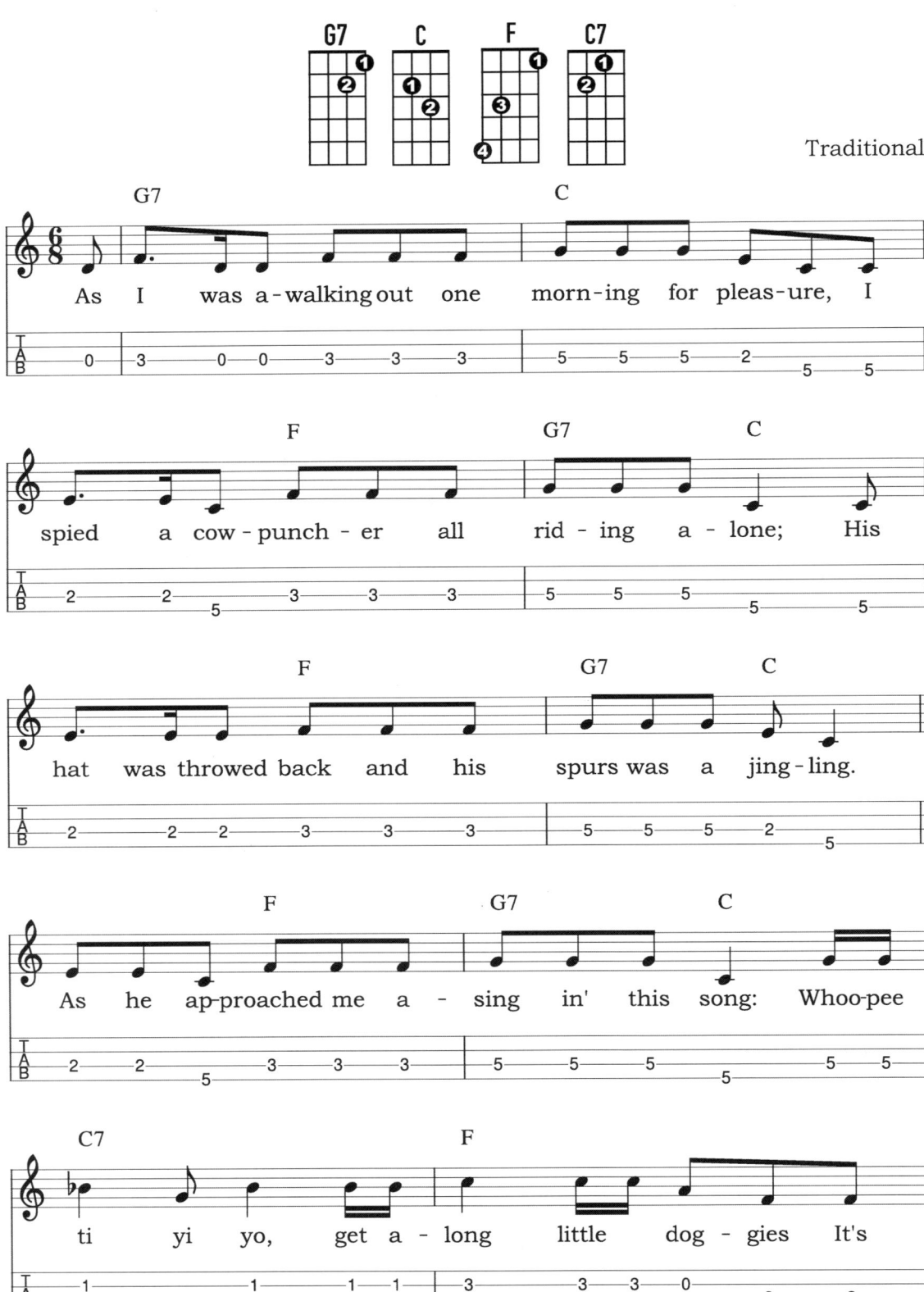

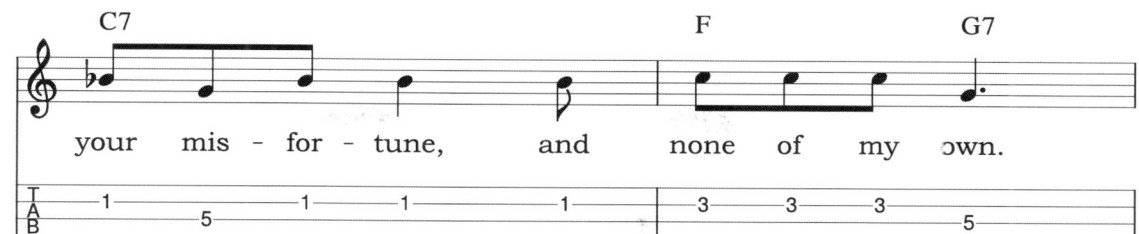

your mis - for - tune,   and   none   of   my   own.

Whoop - ee ti yi yo,   get a - long   lit - tle dogi - es,   For you

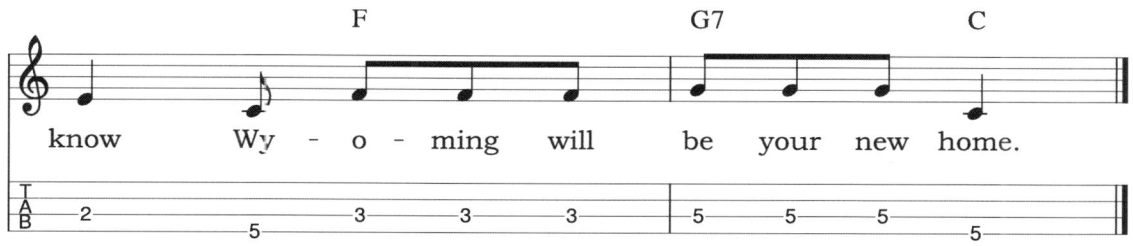

know   Wy - o - ming   will   be   your   new   home.

27

As I was a-walkin out one morning for pleasure,
I spied a cow-puncher all riding alone;
His hat was throwed back and his spurs was a jingling,
As he approached me a-singin' this song:

Chorus:
Whoopee ti yi yo, get along little dogies,
It's your misfortune, and none of my own.
Whoopee ti yi yo, git along little dogies,
For you know Wyoming will be your new home.

Early in the spring we round up the dogies,
Mark and brand and bob off their tails;
Round up our horses, load up the chuck-wagon.
Then throw the dogies upon the trail.

It's whooping and yelling and driving the dogies;
Oh how I wish you would go on;
It's whooping and punching and go on little dogies,
For you know Wyoming will be your new home.

Some boys goes up the trail for pleasure,
But that's where you get it most awfully wrong;
For you haven't any idea the trouble they give us
While we go driving them all along.   *Cont.*

When the night comes on and we hold them on the bedground,
These little dogies that roll on so slow;
Roll up the herd and cut out the strays,
And roll the little dogies that never rolled before.

Your mother she was raised way down in Texas,
Where the jimson weed and sand-burrs grow;
Now we'll fill you up on prickly pear and cholla
Till you are ready for the trail to Idaho.

Oh, you'll be soup for Uncle Sam's Injuns;
"It's beef, heap beef," I hear them cry..
Get along, get along, get along little dogies
You're going to be beef steers by and by.

28

Good-Bye Old Paint

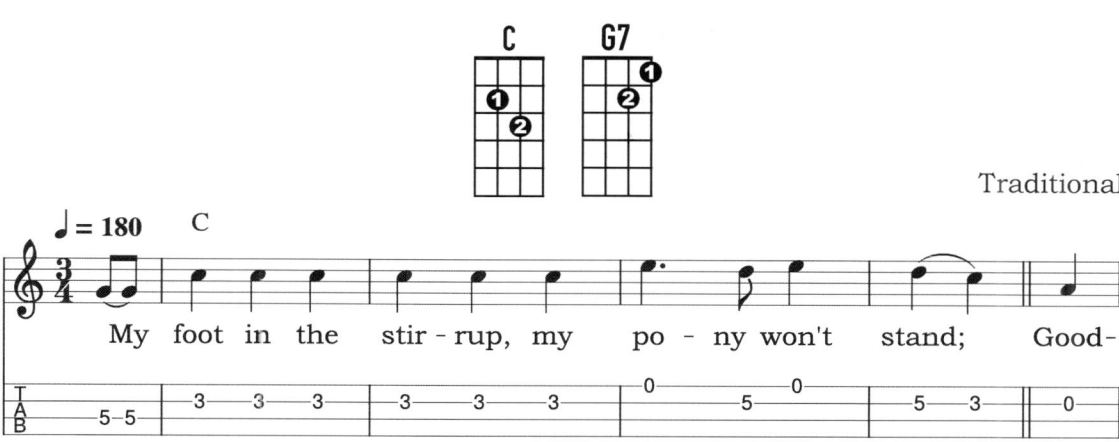

Traditional

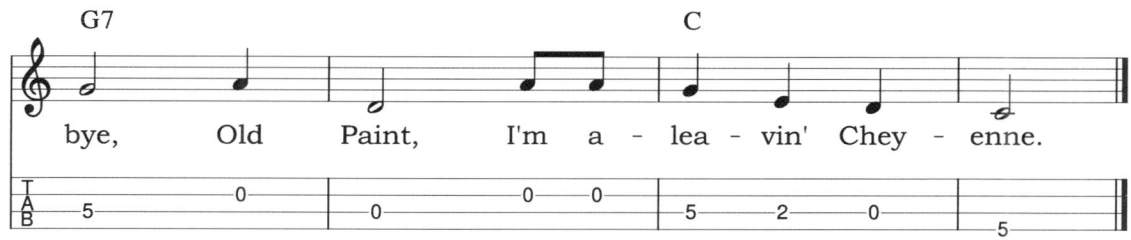

My foot in the stirrup, my pony won't stand;
Goodbye, Old Paint, I'm a-leavin' Cheyenne,
Goodbye, Old Paint, I'm a-leavin' Cheyenne.

I'm a-leavin' Cheyenne, I'm off for Montan';
Goodbye, Old Paint, I'm a-leavin' Cheyenne,
Goodbye, Old Paint, I'm a-leavin' Cheyenne.

I'm a ridin' Old Paint, I'm a-leadin' old Fan;
Goodbye, Old Paint, I'm a-leavin' Cheyenne,
Goodbye, Old Paint, I'm a-leavin' Cheyenne.

With my feet in the stirrups, my bridle in my hand;
Goodbye, Old Paint, I'm a-leavin' Cheyenne,
Goodbye, Old Paint, I'm a-leavin' Cheyenne.

Old Paint's a good pony, he paces when he can;
Goodbye, Old Paint, I'm a-leavin' Cheyenne,
Goodbye, Old Paint, I'm a-leavin' Cheyenne.

Oh, hitch up your horses and feed 'em some hay,
And seat yourself by me so long as you stay.
And seat yourself by me so long as you stay.

My Horses ain't hungry, they'll not eat your hay;
My wagon is loaded and rolling away.
My wagon is loaded and rolling away.

My foot in my stirrup, my reins in my hand;
Good-morning, young lady, my horses won't stand.
Good-morning, young lady, my horses won't stand.

Go, Tell It on the Mountain

Traditional

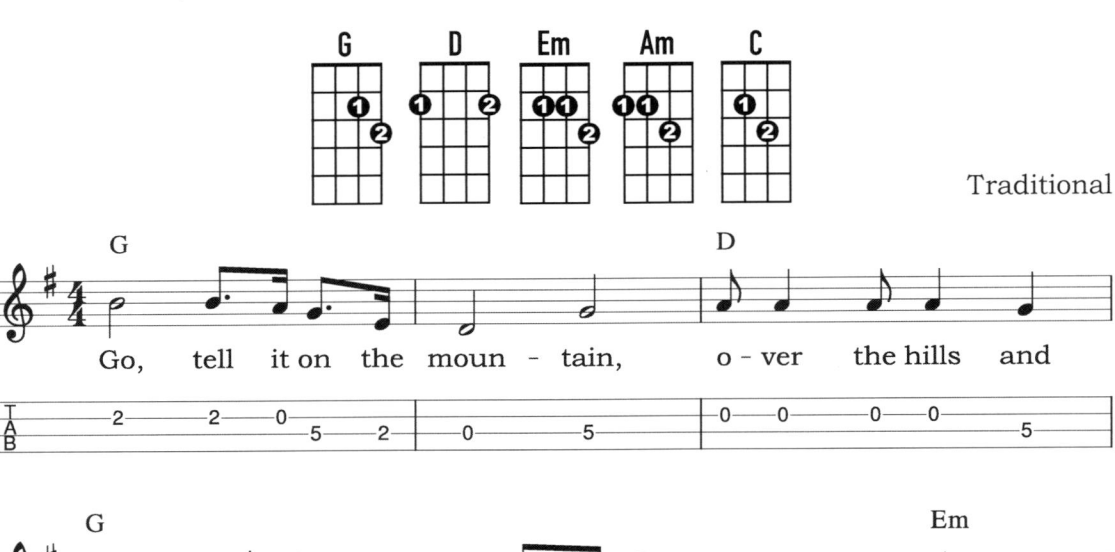

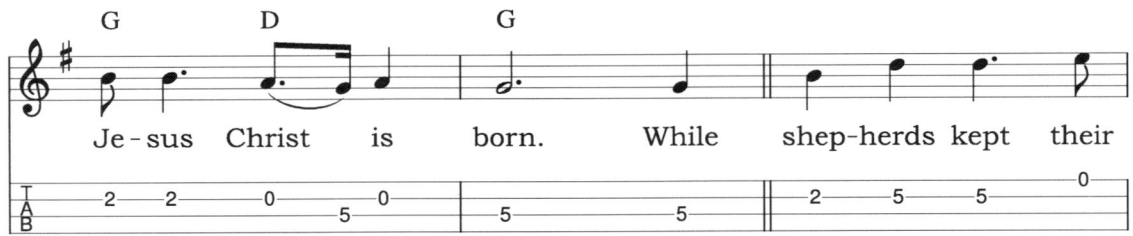

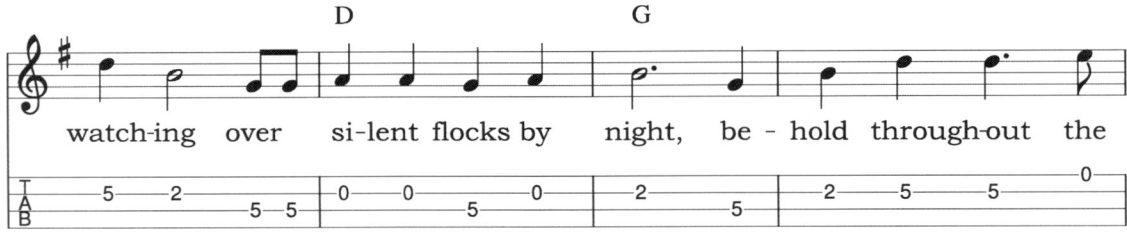

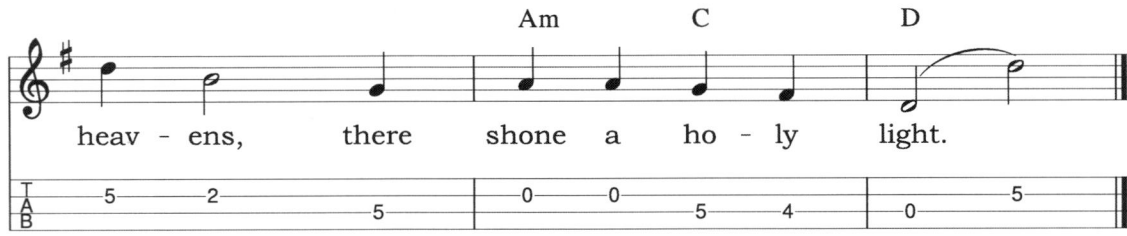

Go, tell it on the mountain,
over the hills and everywhere.
Go, tell it on the mountain
that Jesus Christ is born.

While shepherds kept their watching
over silent flocks by night,
behold throughout the heavens,
there shone a holy light.

Go, tell it on the mountain,
over the hills and everywhere.
Go, tell it on the mountain
that Jesus Christ is born.

The shepherds feared and trembled
when lo, above the earth
rang out the angel chorus
that hailed our Saviour's birth.

Go, tell it on the mountain,
over the hills and everywhere.
Go, tell it on the mountain
that Jesus Christ is born.

Down in a lowly manger
our humble Christ was born,
and God sent us salvation,
that blessed Christmas morn.

Go, tell it on the mountain,
over the hills and everywhere.
Go, tell it on the mountain
that Jesus Christ is born.

Goodnight, Ladies

Traditional

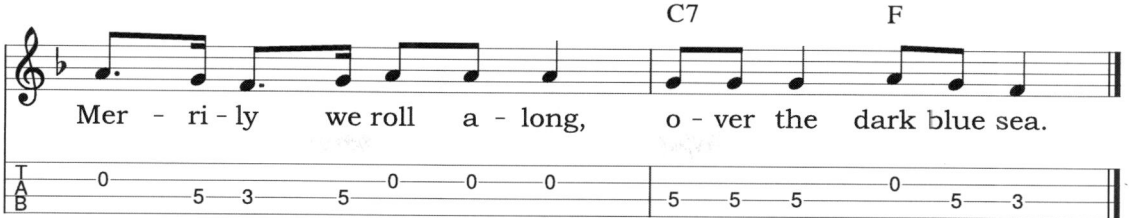

Merrily we roll along, over the dark blue sea.

Good-night, ladies! Good-night, ladies!
Good-night, ladies!
We're going to leave you now.

Chorus:
Merrily we roll along,
Roll along, roll along.
Merrily we roll along,
Over the dark blue sea.

Farewell, ladies! Farewell, ladies!
Farewell, ladies!
We're going to leave you now.

Merrily we roll along,
Roll along, roll along.
Merrily we roll along,
Over the dark blue sea.

Sweet dreams, ladies! Sweet dreams,
ladies! Sweet dreams, ladies!
We're going to leave you now.

Merrily we roll along,
Roll along, roll along.
Merrily we roll along,
Over the dark blue sea.

Hallelujah, I'm a Bum

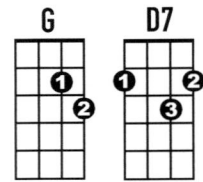

Traditional

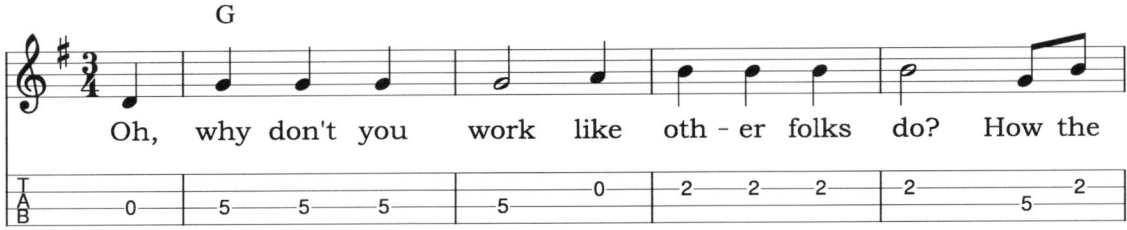

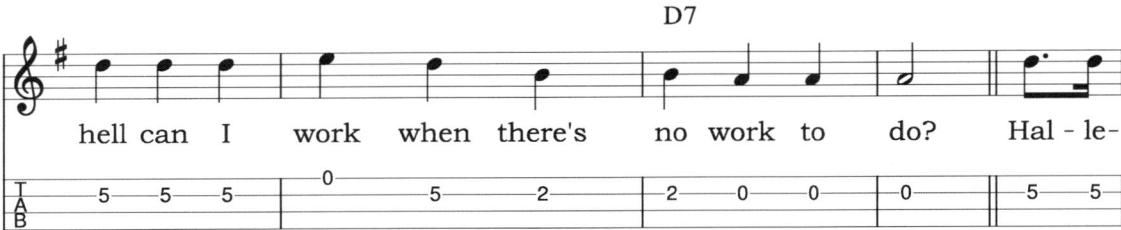

34

Oh, Why don't you work like other folks do?
How the hell can I work when there's no work to do?

Hallelujah, I'm a bum,
Hallelujah, bum again,
Hallelujah, give us a handout
To revive us again.

Oh, why don't you save all the money you earn?
If I didn't eat, I'd have money to burn.

Hallelujah, I'm a bum,
Hallelujah, bum again,
Hallelujah, give us a handout
To revive us again.

Whenever I get all the money I earn,
The boss will be broke, and to work he must turn.

Hallelujah, I'm a bum,
Hallelujah, bum again,
Hallelujah, give us a handout
To revive us again.

Oh, I like my boss, he's a good friend of mine,
That's why I am starving out on the bread line.

Hallelujah, I'm a bum,
Hallelujah, bum again,
Hallelujah, give us a handout
To revive us again.

When springtime it comes, oh, won't we have fun;
We'll throw off our jobs, and go on the bum.

Hallelujah, I'm a bum,
Hallelujah, bum again,
Hallelujah, give us a handout
To revive us again.

Home on the Range

Oh, give me a home where the buffalo roam,
Where the deer and the antelope play,
Where seldom is heard a discouraging word
And the skies are not cloudy all day.

Home, home on the range,
Where the deer and the antelope play;
Where seldom is heard a discouraging word
And the skies are not cloudy all day.

Where the air is so pure, the zephyrs so free,
The breezes so balmy and light,
That I would not exchange my home on the range
For all of the cities so bright.

The red man was pressed from this part of the West,
He's likely no more to return
To the banks of Red River where seldom if ever
Their flickering camp-fires burn.

How often at night when the heavens are bright
With the light from the glittering stars,
Have I stood here amazed and asked as I gazed
If their glory exceeds that of ours.

Oh, I love these wild flowers in this dear land of ours,
The curlew I love to hear scream,
And I love the white rocks and the antelope flocks
That graze on the mountain-tops green.

Oh, give me a land where the bright diamond sand
Flows leisurely down the stream;
Where the graceful white swan goes gliding along
Like a maid in a heavenly dream.

Then I would not exchange my home on the range,
Where the deer and the antelope play;
Where seldom is heard a discouraging word
And the skies are not cloudy all day.

Home, home on the range,
Where the deer and the antelope play;
Where seldom is heard a discouraging word
And the skies are not cloudy all day.

Kumbaya

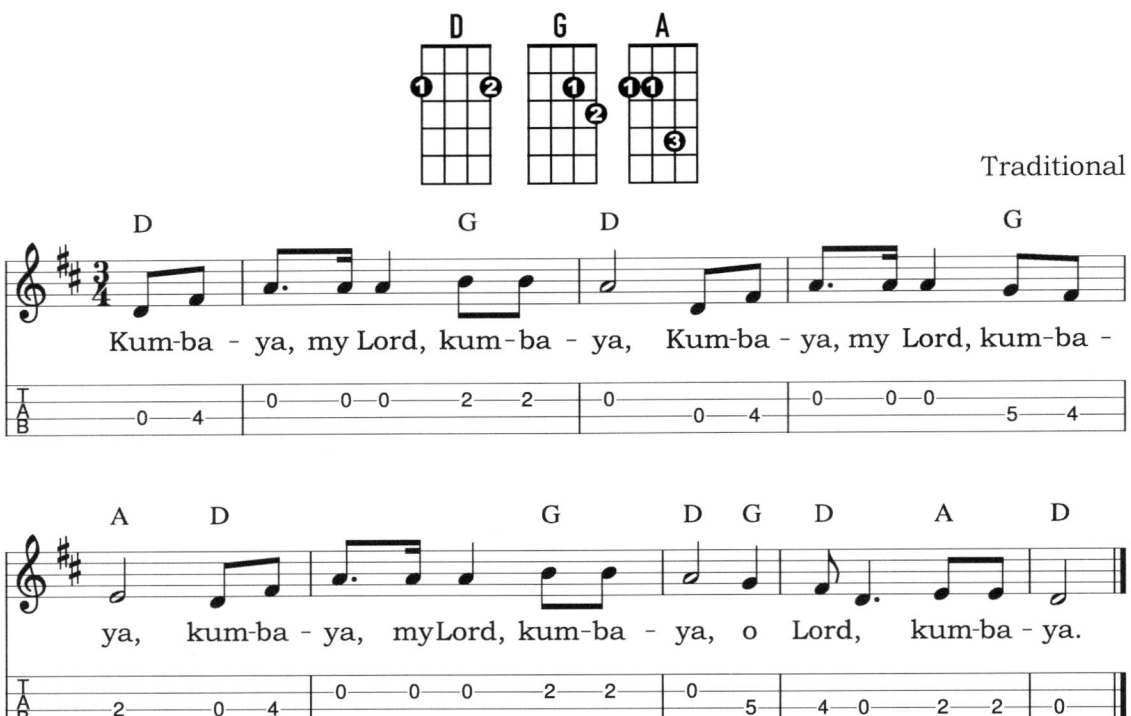

Traditional

Kum-ba - ya, my Lord, kum-ba - ya, Kum-ba - ya, my Lord, kum-ba -

ya, kum-ba - ya, myLord, kum-ba - ya, o Lord, kum-ba - ya.

38

Someone's laughing, Lord, kum bay ya;
Someone's laughing, Lord, kum bay ya;
Someone's laughing, Lord, kum bay ya,
O Lord, kum bay ya.

Someone's crying, Lord, kum bay ya;
Someone's crying, Lord, kum bay ya;
Someone's crying, Lord, kum bay ya,
O Lord, kum bay ya.

Someone's praying, Lord, kum bay ya;
Someone's praying, Lord, kum bay ya;
Someone's praying, Lord, kum bay ya,
O Lord, kum bay ya.

Someone's singing, Lord, kum bay ya;
Someone's singing, Lord, kum bay ya;
Someone's singing, Lord, kum bay ya,
O Lord, kum bay ya.

Li'l Liza Jane

Traditional

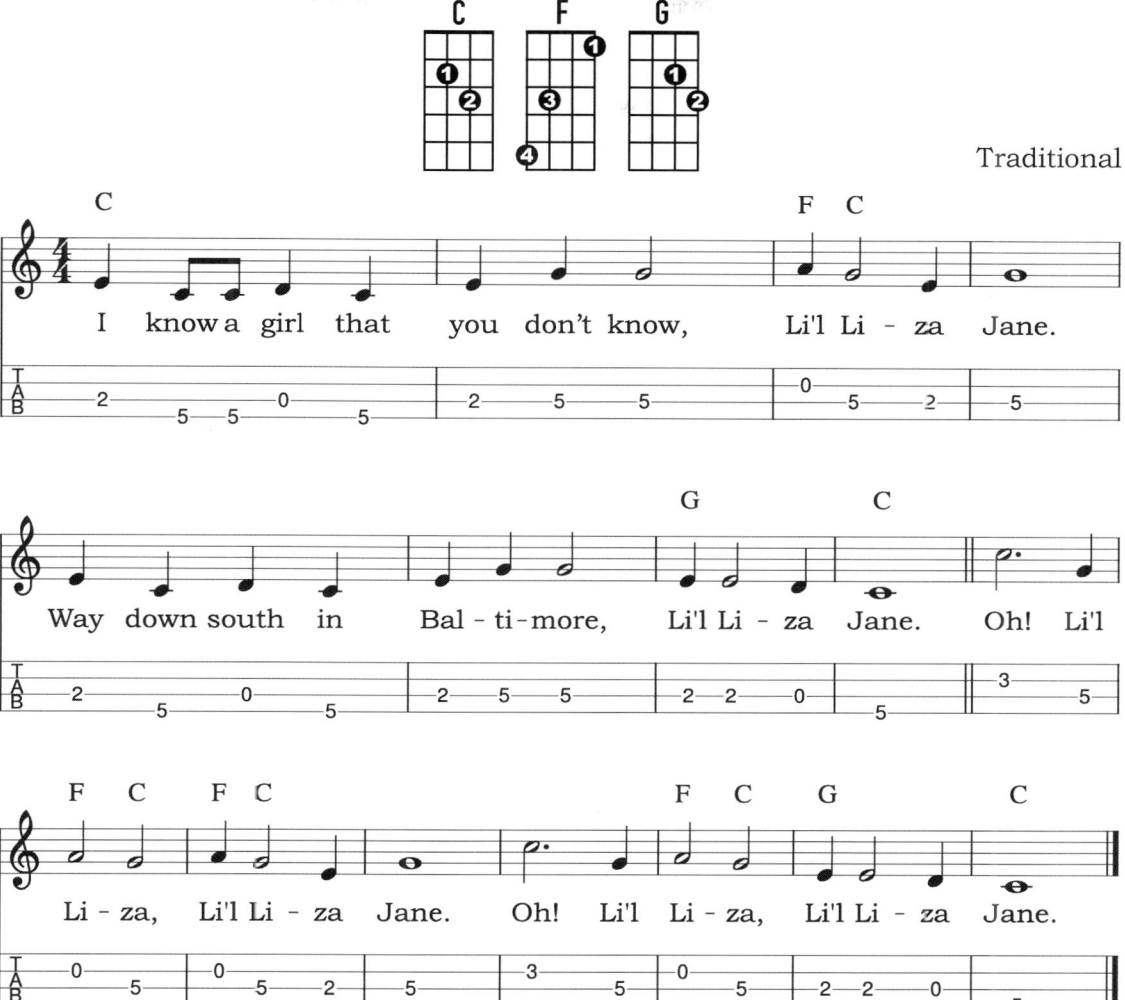

I know a girl that you don't know, Li'l Li - za Jane.

Way down south in Bal - ti - more, Li'l Li - za Jane. Oh! Li'l

Li - za, Li'l Li - za Jane. Oh! Li'l Li - za, Li'l Li - za Jane.

39

Little Brown Jug

Traditional

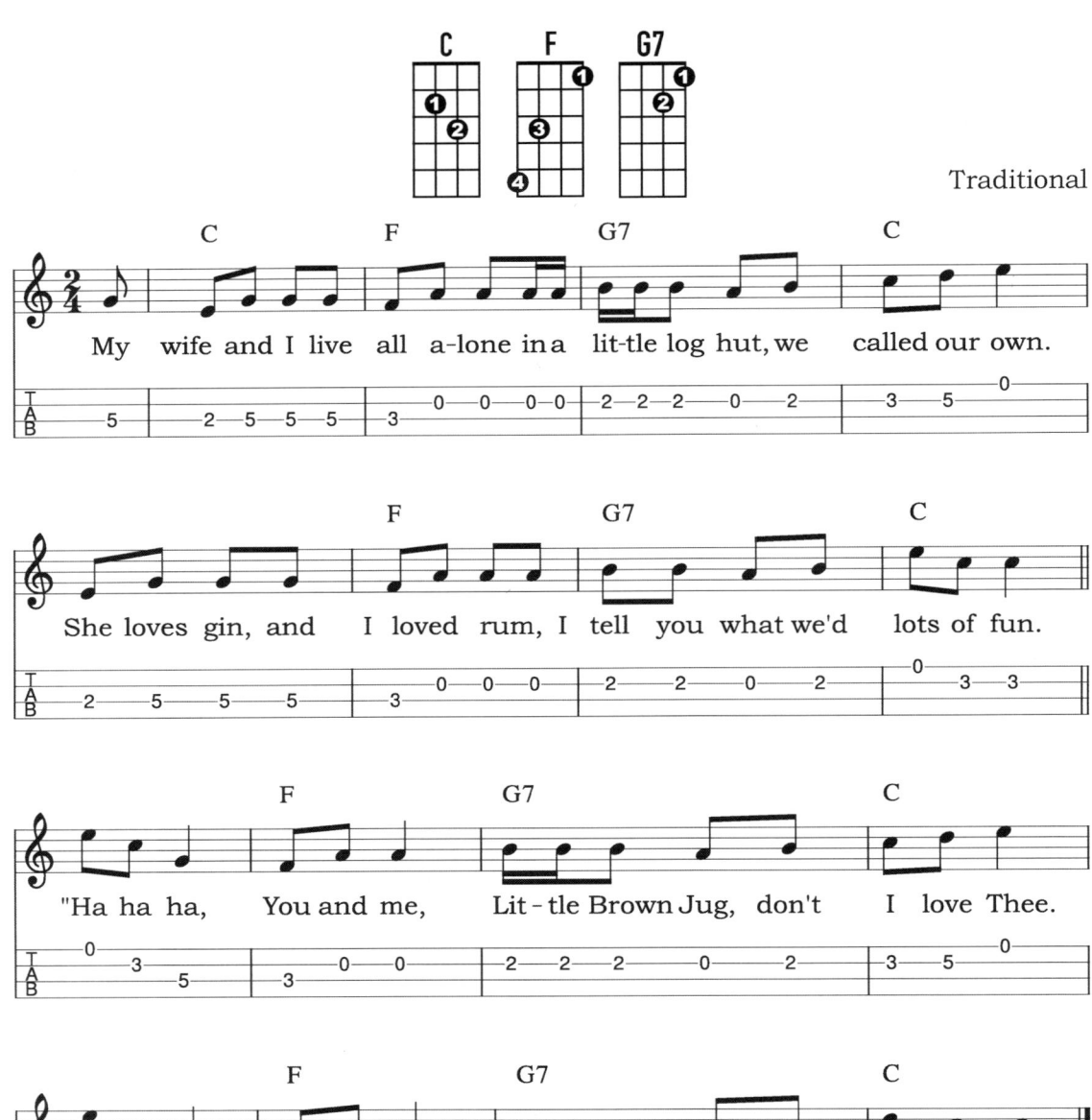

My wife and I live all a-lone in a lit-tle log hut, we called our own.

She loves gin, and I loved rum, I tell you what we'd lots of fun.

"Ha ha ha, You and me, Lit-tle Brown Jug, don't I love Thee.

Ha ha ha, You and me, Lit-tle Brown Jug, don't I love Thee!"

40

My wife and I live all alone
In a little hut we called our own;
She loves gin and I love rum,
I tell you what, we have lots of fun!

Ha, ha, ha, you and me,
Little brown jug, don't I love thee!
Ha, ha, ha, you and me,
Little brown jug, don't I love thee!

'Tis you that makes my friends and foes,
'Tis you that makes me wear old clothes;
But here you are so near my nose,
So tip her up and down she goes.

Ha, ha, ha, you and me,
Little brown jug, don't I love thee!
Ha, ha, ha, you and me,
Little brown jug, don't I love thee!

When I go toiling on my farm
I take the little jug under my arm;
I place it 'neath a shady tree,
Little brown jug, 'tis you and me.

Ha, ha, ha, you and me,
Little brown jug, don't I love thee!
Ha, ha, ha, you and me,
Little brown jug, don't I love thee!

If all the folks in Adam's race
Were gathered together in one place,
I'd let them go without a tear
Before I'd part from you, my dear.

Ha, ha, ha, you and me,
Little brown jug, don't I love thee!
Ha, ha, ha, you and me,
Little brown jug, don't I love thee!

If I'd a cow that gave such milk,
I'd dress her in the finest silk;
Feed her on the choicest hay,
And milk her forty times a day.

Ha, ha, ha, you and me,
Little brown jug, don't I love thee!
Ha, ha, ha, you and me,
Little brown jug, don't I love thee!

I bought a cow from Farmer Jones,
And she was nothing but skin and bones;
I fed her up as fine as silk,
She jumped the fence and strained her milk.

Ha, ha, ha, you and me,
Little brown jug, don't I love thee!
Ha, ha, ha, you and me,
Little brown jug, don't I love thee!

And when I die don't bury me at all,
Just pickle my bones in alcohol;
Put a bottle o' booze at my head and feet
And then I know that I will keep.

Ha, ha, ha, you and me,
Little brown jug, don't I love thee!
Ha, ha, ha, you and me,
Little brown jug, don't I love thee!

The rose is red, my nose is too,
The violet's blue and so are you;
And yet, I guess, before I stop,
We'd better take another drop.

Ha, ha, ha, you and me,
Little brown jug, don't I love thee!
Ha, ha, ha, you and me,
Little brown jug, don't I love thee!

Long, Long Ago

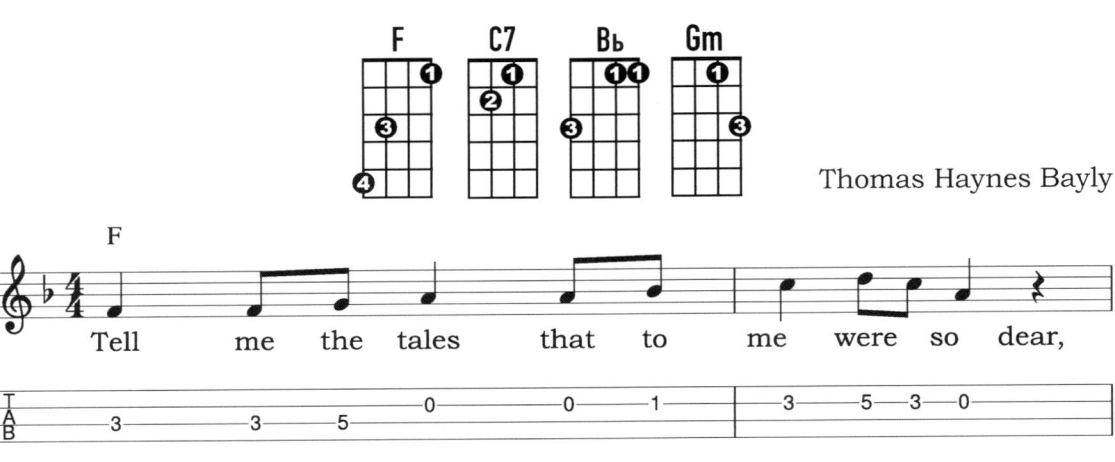

Thomas Haynes Bayly

Tell me the tales that to me were so dear,

long, long a-go, long, long a-go. Sing me the songs I de-

42

light - ed to hear, Long, long a - go long a - go.

Now you are come, all my grief is re-mov'd.

Let me for - get that so long you have rov'd,

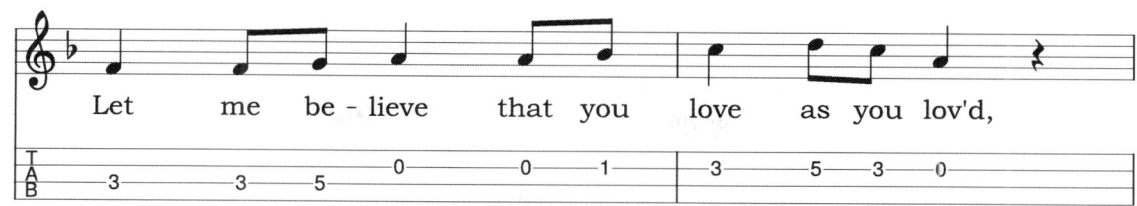

Let me be-lieve that you love as you lov'd,

C7   F

Long, long a - go, long, a - go.

Tell me the tales that to me were so dear,
Long, long ago, long, long ago:
Sing me the songs I delighted to hear,
Long, long ago long ago.
Now you are come, all my grief is remov'd,
Let me forget that so long you have rov'd,
Let me believe that you love as you lov'd,
Long, long ago, long ago.

Do you remember the path where we met,
Long long ago, long long ago.
Ah yes you told me you ne'er would forget,
Long long ago, long ago.
Then to all others my smile you prefer'd,
Love when you spoke gave a charm to each word,
Still my heart treasures the praises I heard,
Long long ago, long ago.

Thought by your kindness my fond hopes were raised,
Long long ago, long long ago,
You by more eloquent lips have been prais'd,
Long long ago, long ago,
But by long absence your truth has been tried,
Still to your accents I listen with pride,
Blest as I was when I sat by your side,
Long long ago, long ago.

Looby Loo

Traditional

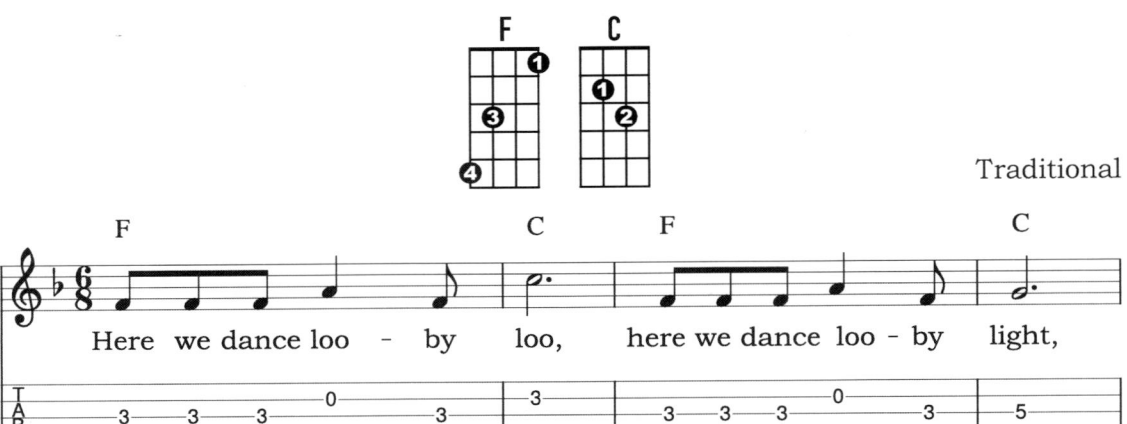

Here we dance loo - by loo, here we dance loo - by light,

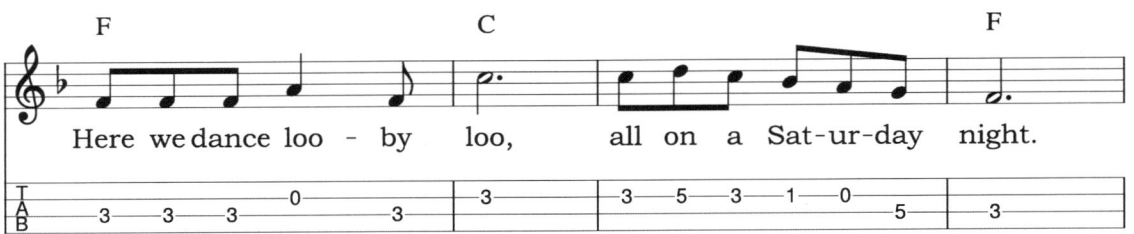

Here we dance loo - by loo, all on a Sat-ur-day night.

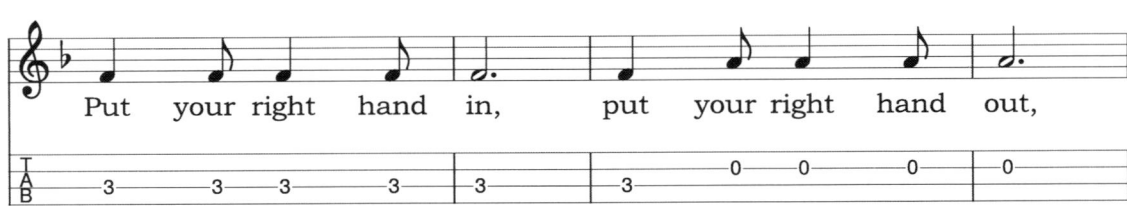

Put your right hand in, put your right hand out,

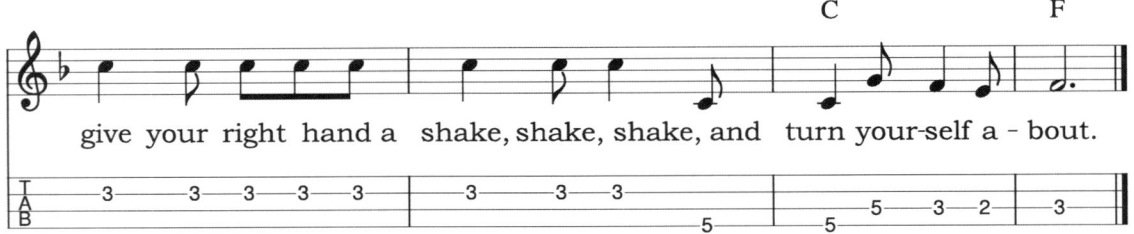

give your right hand a shake, shake, shake, and turn your-self a - bout.

Here we dance looby loo,
Here we dance looby light,
Here we dance looby loo,
All on a Saturday night.

Put your right hand in.
Put your right hand out.
Give your right hand a shake, shake, shake,
And turn yourself about.

Here we dance looby loo,
Here we dance looby light,
Here we dance looby loo,
All on a Saturday night.

Put your left hand in.
Put your left hand out.
Give your left hand a shake, shake, shake,
And turn yourself about.

Here we dance looby loo,
Here we dance looby light,
Here we dance looby loo,
All on a Saturday night.

Put your right foot in.
Put your right foot out.
Give your right foot a shake, shake, shake,
And turn yourself about.

Here we dance looby loo,
Here we dance looby light,
Here we dance looby loo,
All on a Saturday night.

Put your left foot in.
Put your left foot out.
Give your left foot a shake, shake, shake,
And turn yourself about.

Here we dance looby loo,
Here we dance looby light,
Here we dance looby loo,
All on a Saturday night.

Put your head 'way in,
Put your head 'way out.
You give your head a shake, shake, shake,
And turn yourself about.

Here we dance looby loo,
Here we dance looby light,
Here we dance looby loo,
All on a Saturday night.

Put your whole self in.
Put your whole self out.
Give your self a shake, shake, shake,
And turn yourself about.

Here we dance looby loo,
Here we dance looby light,
Here we dance looby loo,
All on a Saturday night.

45

Michael, Row the Boat Ashore

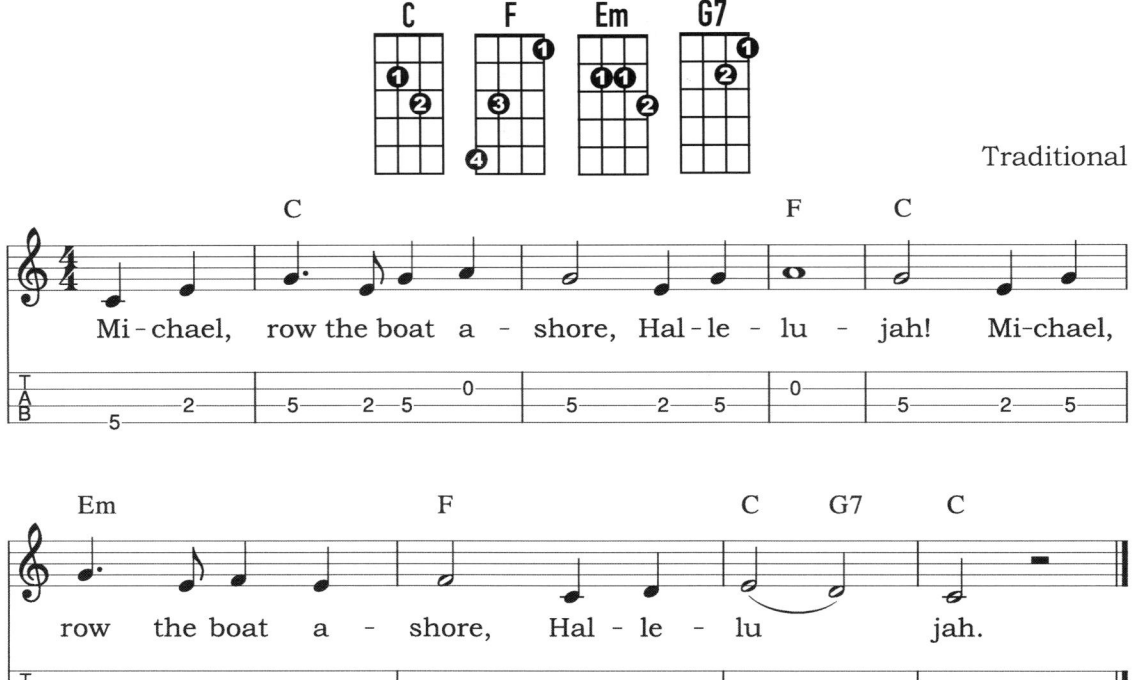

Traditional

Mi-chael, row the boat a - shore, Hal-le-lu - jah! Mi-chael,

row the boat a - shore, Hal-le-lu jah.

46

Michael, row the boat ashore, Hallelujah.
Michael, row the boat ashore, Hallelujah.

Brother lend a helping hand, Hallelujah,
Brother lend a helping hand, Hallelujah.

Children, sing a sailor song, Hallelujah.
Children, call the boat back home. Hallelujah.

Sister, help to trim the sail, Hallelujah.
Sister, help to trim the sail, Hallelujah.

Michael, haul the boat ashore, Hallelujah.
Michael, stay forever more, Hallelujah.

Old Texsas

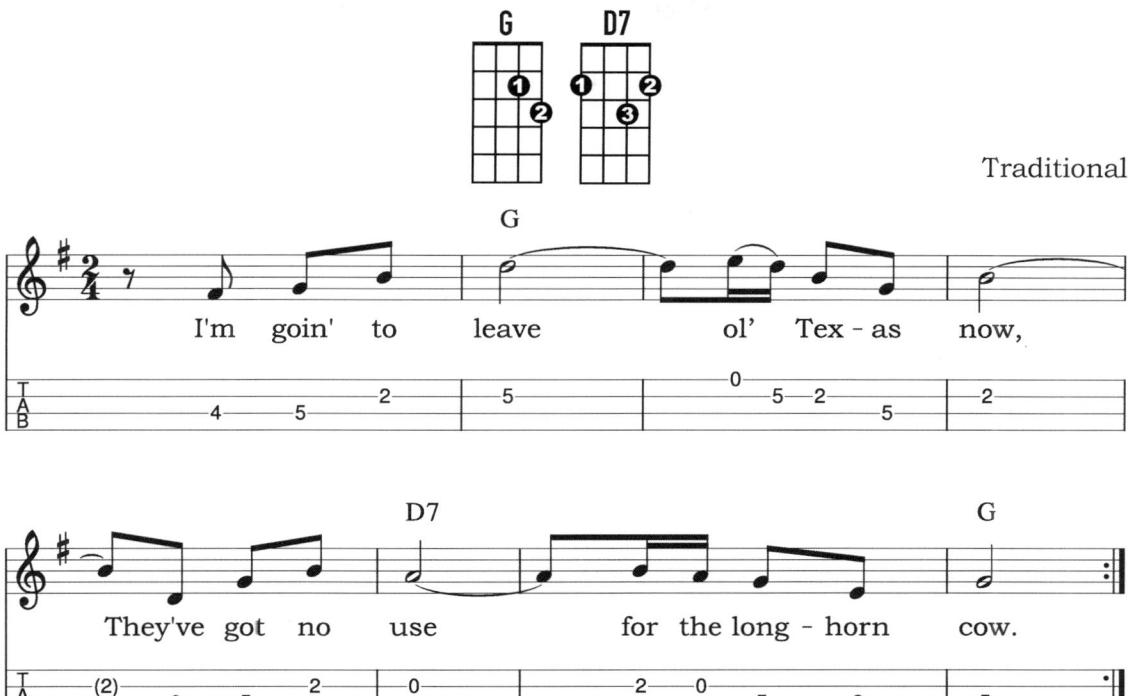

Traditional

I'm goin' to leave ol' Tex - as now,

They've got no use for the long - horn cow.

I'm going to leave ol' Texas now,
They've got no use for the longhorn cow,
They've plowed and fenced all o'er the range,
And the people there are all so strange.

I'll take my horse, I'll take my rope,
And I'll hit the ground upon a lope,
I'll bid adieu to the Alamo,
And I'll turn my head to Mexico.

The cold hard ground will be my bed,
And the saddle seat will hold my head,
And when I wake up from my dreams,
I'll eat some bread and a pan of beans.

And when my ride on Earth is done,
I'll take my chance with the Holy One,
And when I die please bury me,
Under the sky on the lone prairie

Oh My Darling, Clementine

Percy Montrose

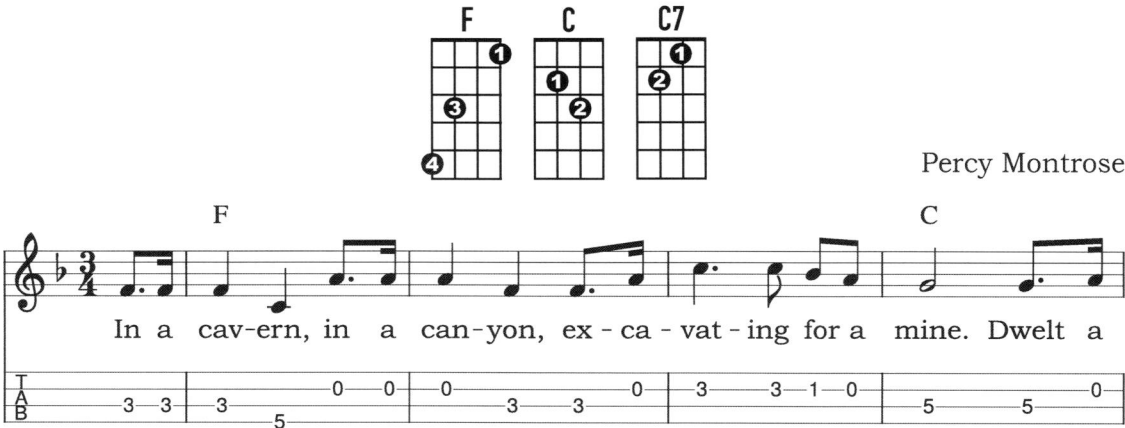

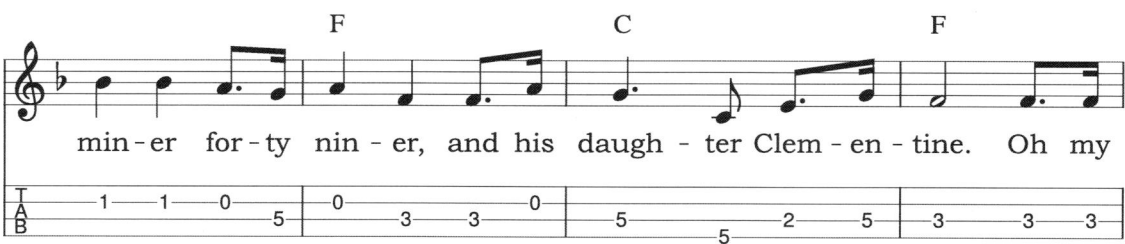

48

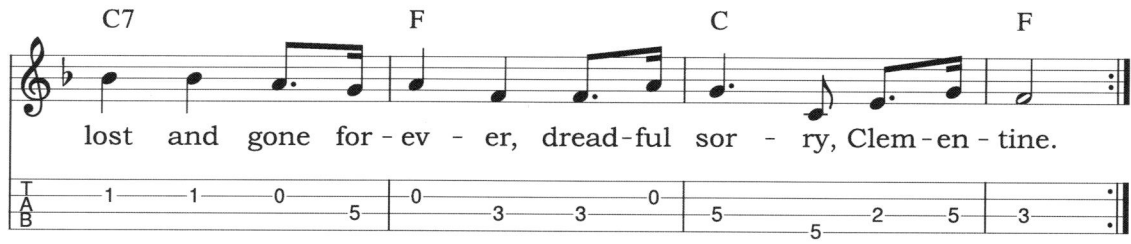

In a cavern, in a canyon,
Excavating for a mine
Dwelt a miner forty-niner,
And his daughter Clementine.

Oh my darling, oh my darling,
Oh my darling, Clementine!
Thou art lost and gone forever
Dreadful sorry, Clementine.

Light she was and like a fairy,
And her shoes were number nine,
Herring boxes, without topses,
Sandals were for Clementine.

Oh my darling, oh my darling,
Oh my darling, Clementine!
Thou art lost and gone forever
Dreadful sorry, Clementine.

Drove she ducklings to the water
Every morning just at nine,
Hit her foot against a splinter,
Fell into the foaming brine.

Oh my darling, oh my darling,
Oh my darling, Clementine!
Thou art lost and gone forever
Dreadful sorry, Clementine.

Ruby lips above the water,
Blowing bubbles, soft and fine,
But, alas, I was no swimmer,
So I lost my Clementine.

Oh my darling, oh my darling,
Oh my darling, Clementine!
Thou art lost and gone forever
Dreadful sorry, Clementine.

How I missed her! How I missed her,
How I missed my Clementine,
But I kissed her little sister,
I forgot my Clementine.

Oh my darling, oh my darling,
Oh my darling, Clementine!
Thou art lost and gone forever
Dreadful sorry, Clementine.

Oh, Susanna

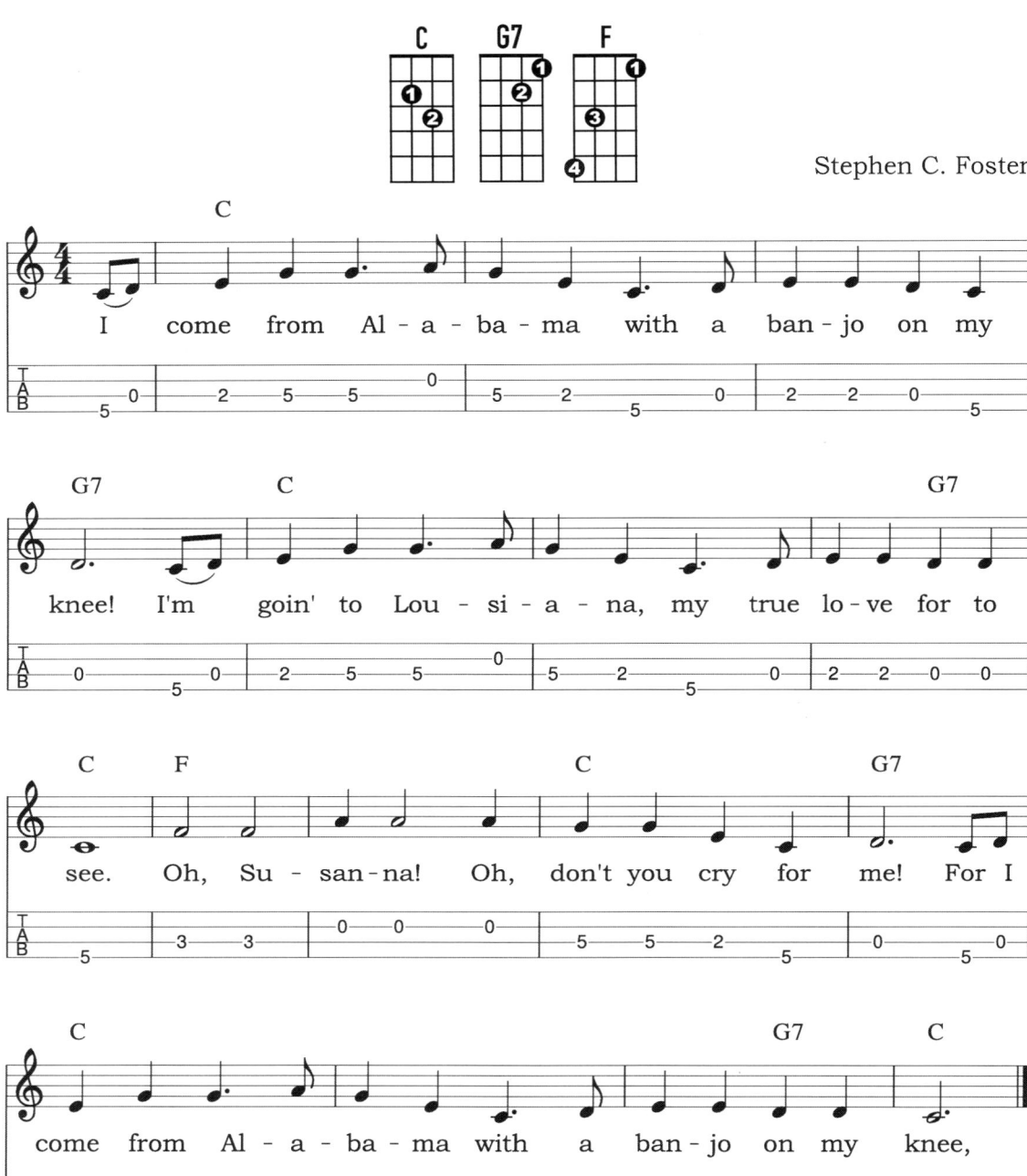

Stephen C. Foster

50

I came from Alabama,
With my banjo on my knee,
I'm going to Louisiana,
My true love for to see;
It rained all night the day I left,
The weather it was dry,
The sun so hot I froze to death,
Susanna, don't you cry.

Oh! Susanna, Oh don't you cry for me,
For I've come from Alabama
With my banjo on my knee.

I had a dream the other night,
When everything was still;
I thought I saw Susanna,
A coming down the hill;
The buckwheat cake was in her mouth,
The tear was in her eye;
Says I, "I'm coming from the south,
Susanna, don't you cry."

Oh! Susanna, Oh don't you cry for me,
For I've come from Alabama
With my banjo on my knee.

I soon will be in New Orleans,
And then I'll look around,
And when I find Susanna,
I'll fall upon the ground.
But if I do not find her,
Then I will surely die,
And when I'm dead and buried,
Oh, Susanna, don't you cry.

Oh! Susanna, Oh don't you cry for me,
For I've come from Alabama
With my banjo on my knee.

Polly Wolly Doodle

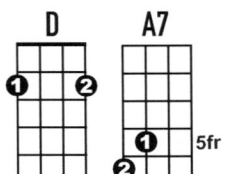

Traditional

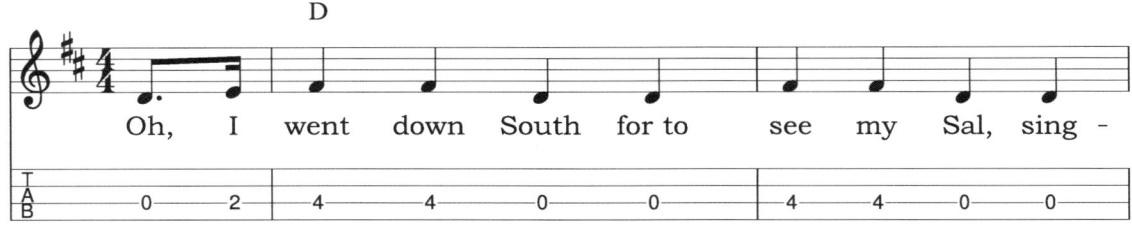

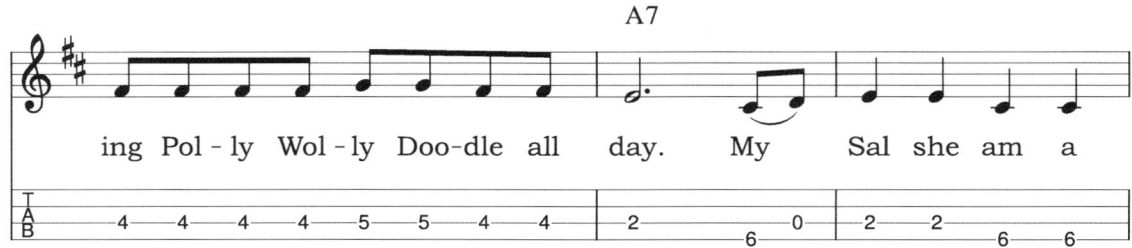

Pol - ly Wol - ly Doo - dle all the day.

Oh, I went down South for to see my Sal,
Singing Polly Wolly Doodle all the day.
My Sal she am a spunky gal,
Singing Polly Wolly Doodle all the day.

Fare thee well, fare thee well,
Fare thee well, my fairy fay,
For I'm goin' to Louisiana for to see my Susyanna,
Sing Polly Wolly Doodle all the day.

Oh, my Sal, she is a maiden fair,
Singing Polly wolly doodle all the day,
With curly eyes And laughing hair,
Singing Polly wolly doodle all the day.

Fare thee well, fare thee well,
Fare thee well, my fairy fay,
For I'm goin' to Louisiana for to see my Susyanna,
Sing Polly Wolly Doodle all the day.

Behind the barn, down on my knees
Singing Polly wolly doodle all the day.
I thought I heard a chicken sneeze,
Singing Polly wolly doodle all the day.

Fare thee well, fare thee well,
Fare thee well, my fairy fay,
For I'm goin' to Louisiana for to see my Susyanna,
Sing Polly Wolly Doodle all the day.

On Top of Old Smoky

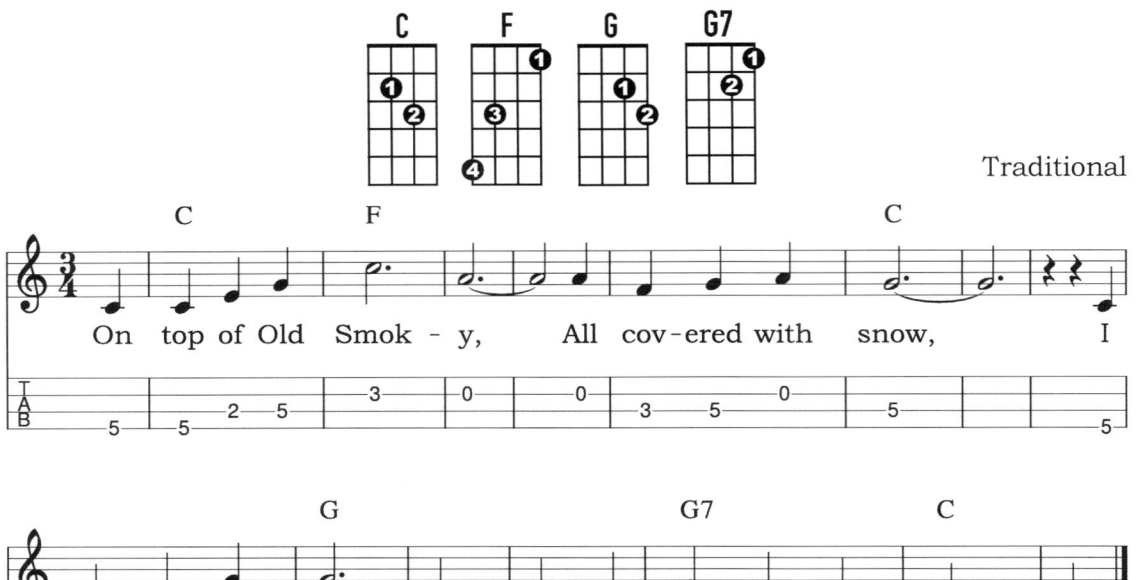

Traditional

On top of Old Smok - y, All cov-ered with snow, I

lost my true lov - er For cour-ting too slow.

54

On top of old smokey
All covered with snow
I lost my true lover
For courting too slow

For courting's a pleasure
And parting's a grief.
And a false hearted lover
Is worse than a thief.

For a thief will just rob you
And take all you save,
But a false hearted lover
Will lead you to the grave.

And the grave will decay you
And turn you to dust.
Not one girl in a hundred
A poor boy can trust.

They'll hug you and kiss you
And tell you more lies.
Than cross lines on a railroad
Or stars in the skies.

So come all your maidens
And listen to me,
Never place your affections
On a green willow tree.

For the leaves they will wither
And the roots they will die.
You'll all be forsaken
And never know why.

Red River Valley

Traditional

From this val - ley they say you are go - ing,

I will miss your bright eyes and sweet smile,

for they say you are tak - ing the sun - shine,

that has bright - ened our path - ways a - while.

From this valley they say you are going.
We will miss your bright eyes and sweet smile,
For they say you are taking the sunshine
That has brightened our pathway a while.

So come sit by my side if you love me.
Do not hasten to bid me adieu.
Just remember the Red River Valley,
And the cowboy that has loved you so true.

Rye Whiskey

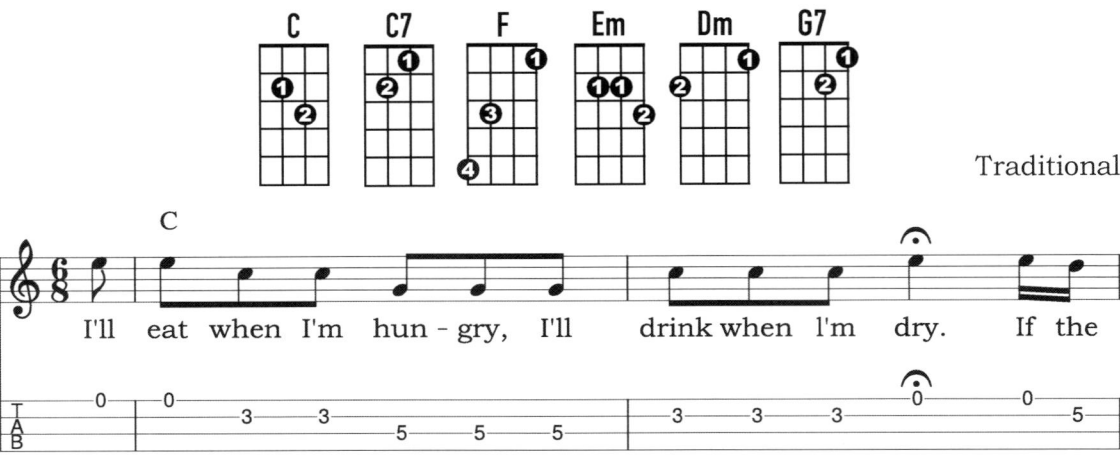

Traditional

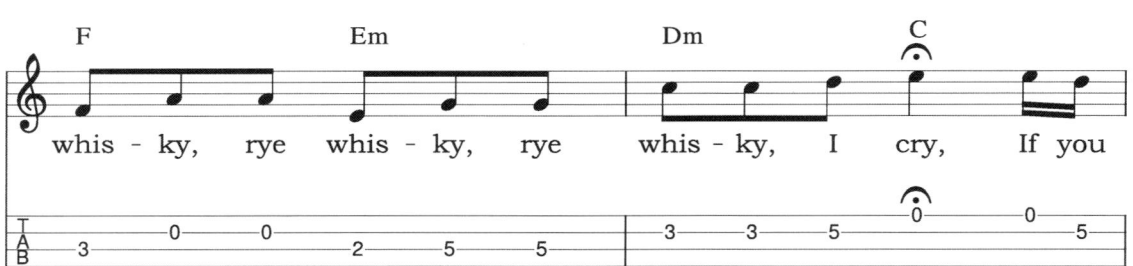

I'll eat when I'm hungry,
I'll drink when I'm dry.
If the hard times don't kill me,
I'll live till I die.

Chorus:
Rye whisky, rye whisky,
Rye whisky, I cry,
If you don't give me rye whisky,
I surely will die.

I'll tune up my fiddle,
And I'll rosin my bow,
I'll make myself welcome,
Wherever I go.

Beefsteak when I'm hungry,
Red liquor when I'm dry,
Greenbacks when I'm hard up,
And religion when I die.

They say I drink whisky,
My money's my own;
All them that don't like me,
Can leave me alone.

Sometimes I drink whisky,
Sometimes I drink rum,
Sometimes I drink brandy,
At other times none.

But if I get boozy,
My whisky's my own,
And them that don't like me,
Can leave me alone.

Jack o' diamonds, jack o' diamonds,
I know you of old,
You've robbed my poor pockets
Of silver and gold.

Oh, whisky, you villain,
You've been my downfall,
You've kicked me, you've cuffed me,
But I love you for all.

If the ocean was whisky,
And I was a duck,
I'd dive to the bottom
To get one sweet suck.

But the ocean ain't whisky
And I ain't a duck,
So we'll round up the cattle
And then we'll get drunk.

My foot's in my stirrup,
My bridle's in my hand,
I'm leaving sweet Lillie,
The fairest in the land.

Her parents don't like me,
They say I'm too poor;
They say I'm unworthy
To enter her door.

Sweet milk when I'm hungry,
Rye whisky when I'm dry,
If a tree don't fall on me,
I'll live till I die.

I'll buy my own whisky,
I'll make my own stew,
If I get drunk, madam,
It's nothing to you.

I'll drink my own whisky,
I'll drink my own wine,
Some ten thousand bottles
I've killed in my time.

I've no wife to quarrel
No babies to bawl;
The best way of living
Is no wife at all.

Way up on Clinch Mountain
I wander alone,
I'm as drunk as the devil,
Oh, let me alone.

You may boast of your knowledge
An' brag of your sense,
'Twill all be forgotten
A hundred years hence.

57

She'll Be Coming 'Round the Mountain

Traditional

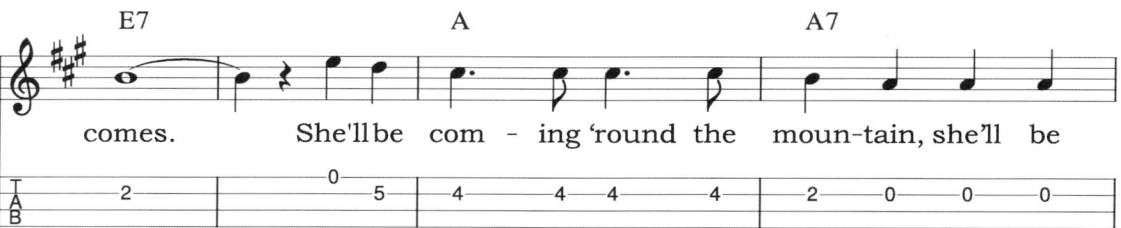

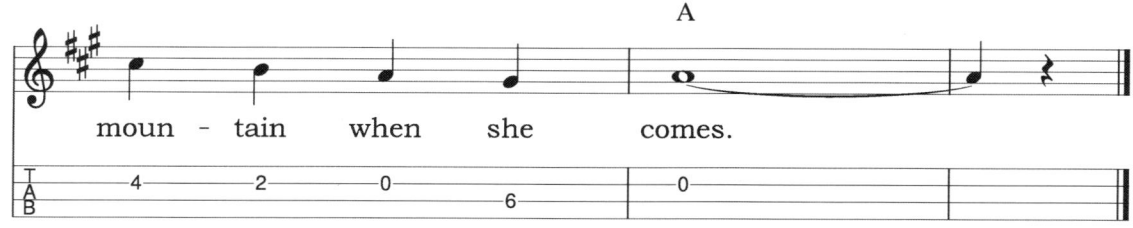

She'll be coming 'round the mountain when she comes.
She'll be coming 'round the mountain when she comes.
She'll be coming 'round the mountain,
she'll be coming 'round the mountain,
she'll be coming 'round the mountain when she comes.

She'll be driving six white horses when she comes.
She'll be driving six white horses when she comes.
She'll be driving six white horses,
she'll be driving six white horses,
she'll be driving six white horses when she comes.

Oh, we'll all go out to meet her when she comes.
Oh, we'll all go out to meet her when she comes.
Oh, we'll all go out to meet her,
Oh, we'll all go out to meet her,
Oh, we'll all go out to meet her when she comes.

Oh, we'll all have chicken and dumplings when she comes.
Oh, we'll all have chicken and dumplings when she comes.
Oh we'll all have chicken and dumplings,
Oh, we'll all have chicken and dumplings,
Oh, we'll all have chicken and dumplings when she comes.

We'll be singing "Hallelujah" when she comes.
We'll be singing "Hallelujah" when she comes.
We'll be singing "Hallelujah,
"We'll be singing "Hallelujah,
"We'll be singing "Hallelujah" when she comes.

Shortnin' Bread

Traditional

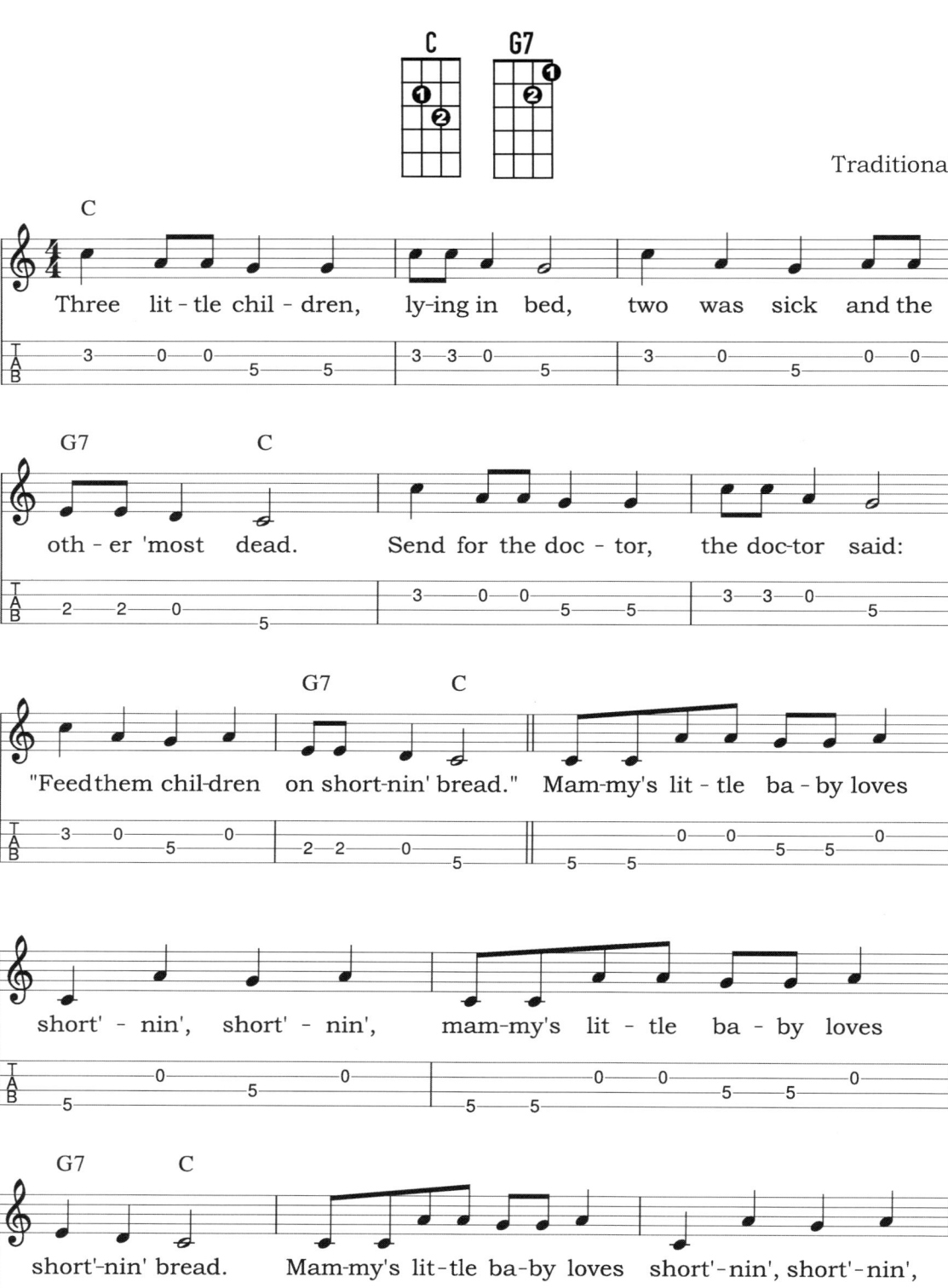

60

Three little children, lying in bed
Two was sick and the other 'most dead
Send for the doctor and the doctor said
"feed them children on short'nin' bread".

Mammy's little baby loves short'nin', short'nin',
Mammy's little baby loves short'nin' bread.

Pull out the skillet, pull out the led,
Mama's gonna make a little short'nin' bread.
That ain't all she's gonna do,
Mama's gonna make a little coffee too.

Mammy's little baby loves short'nin', short'nin',
Mammy's little baby loves short'nin' bread.

I slipped to the kitchen, slipped on the led,
slipped my pockets full of short'nin' bread.
I stole the skillet, I stole the led,
I stole the girl who makes short'nin' bread.

Mammy's little baby loves short'nin', short'nin',
Mammy's little baby loves short'nin' bread.

They caught me with the skillet, They caught me with the led,
They caught me with the girl who makes short'nin' bread.
I paid six dollars for the skillet, six dollars for the led,
Spent six months in jail eating short'nin' bread.

Simple Gifts

Joseph Brackett

'Tis the gift to be sim-ple, 'tis the gift to be free. 'Tis the gift to come down where we ought to be, and

when we find our-selves in the place just right, 'twill

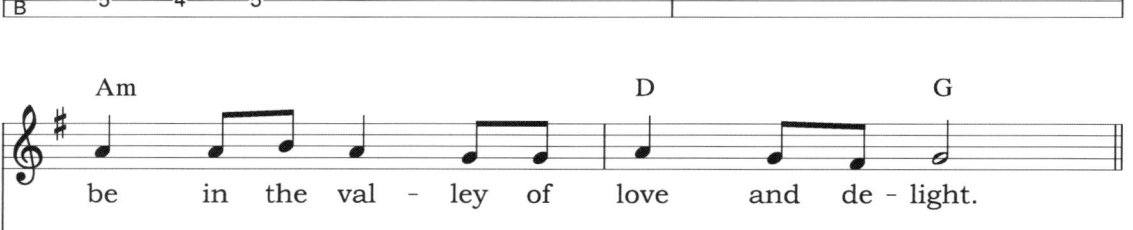

be in the val - ley of love and de - light.

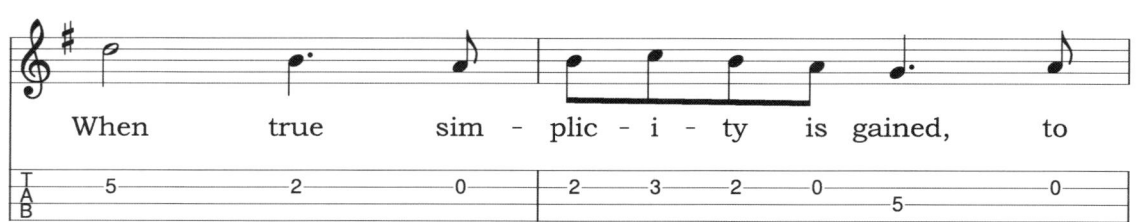

When true sim - plic - i - ty is gained, to

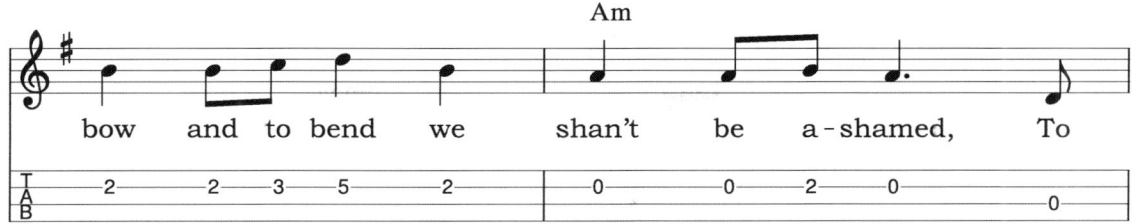

bow   and to bend   we   shan't   be   a-shamed,   To

turn,   turn   will   be   our   de - light,   Till   by

turn - ing,   turn - ing we   come   'round   right.

Tis the gift to be simple, 'tis the gift to be free
'Tis the gift to come down where we ought to be,
And when we find ourselves in the place just right,
'Twill be in the valley of love and delight.

Chorus:
When true simplicity is gained,
To bow and to bend we shan't be ashamed,
To turn, turn will be our delight,
Till by turning, turning we come 'round right.

Tis the gift to be loved and that love to return,
'Tis the gift to be taught and a richer gift to learn,
And when we expect of others what we try to live each day,
Then we'll all live together and we'll all learn to say.

Chorus

'Tis the gift to have friends and a true friend to be,
'Tis the gift to think of others not to only think of "me",
And when we hear what others really think and really feel,
Then we'll all live together with a love that is real.

Chorus

Shady Grove

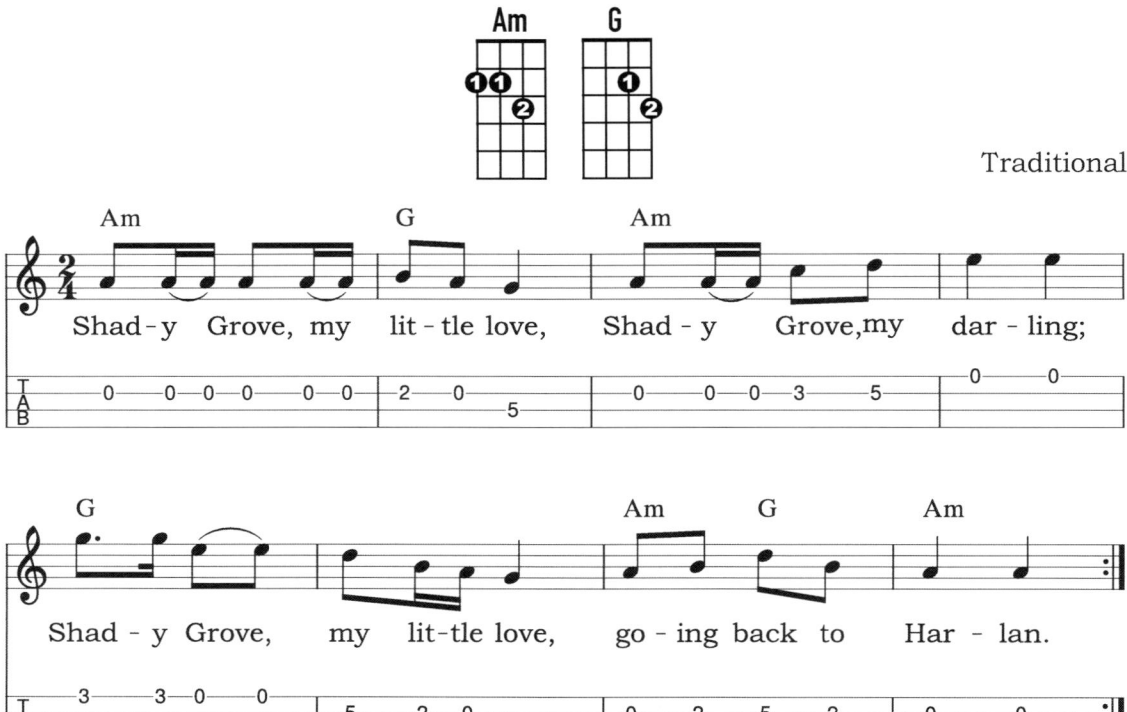

Traditional

Shady grove, my little love,
Shady grove, my darling;
Shady grove, my little love,
Going back to Harlan.

Fly around, my blue-eyed girl,
Fly around, my daisy;
Fly around, my blue-eyed girl;
Nearly drive me crazy.

The very next time I go that road.
And it don't look so dark and grazy;
The very next time I come that road,
Stop and see my daisy.

I once had a mulie cow,
Mulie when she was born;
Took a jay-bird forty year
To fly from horn to horn.

Apples in the summer.
Peaches in the fall;
If I can't marry the girl I want,
I won't have none at all.

Skip to My Lou

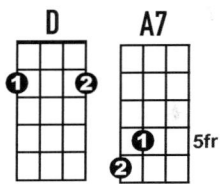

Traditional

Skip, skip, skip to my Lou, skip, skip, skip to my Lou,

skip, skip, skip to my Lou, skip to my Lou, my dar - ling.

Skip, skip, skip to my Lou,
Skip, skip, skip to my Lou,
Skip, skip, skip to my Lou,
Skip to my Lou, my darlin'.

Lou, Lou skip to my Lou,
Lou, Lou skip to my Lou,
Lou, Lou skip to my Lou,
Skip to my Lou my darlin'.

Fly in the buttermilk, shoo, fly, shoo.
Fly in the buttermilk, shoo, fly, shoo.
Fly in the buttermilk, shoo, fly, shoo.
Skip to my Lou, my darlin'.

Lou, Lou skip to my Lou,
Lou, Lou skip to my Lou,
Lou, Lou skip to my Lou,
Skip to my Lou my darlin'.

There's a little red wagon, paint it blue.
There's a little red wagon, paint it blue.
There's a little red wagon, paint it blue.
Skip to my Lou, my darlin'.

Lou, Lou skip to my Lou,
Lou, Lou skip to my Lou,
Lou, Lou skip to my Lou,
Skip to my Lou my darlin'.

I lost my partner, what'll I do?
I lost my partner, what'll I do?
I lost my partner, what'll I do?
Skip to my Lou, my darlin'.

Lou, Lou skip to my Lou,
Lou, Lou skip to my Lou,
Lou, Lou skip to my Lou,
Skip to my Lou my darlin'.

I'll get another, as pretty as you.
I'll get another, as pretty as you.
I'll get another, as pretty as you.
Skip to my Lou, my darlin'.

Lou, Lou skip to my Lou,
Lou, Lou skip to my Lou,
Lou, Lou skip to my Lou,
Skip to my Lou my darlin'.

Swing Low Sweet Chariot

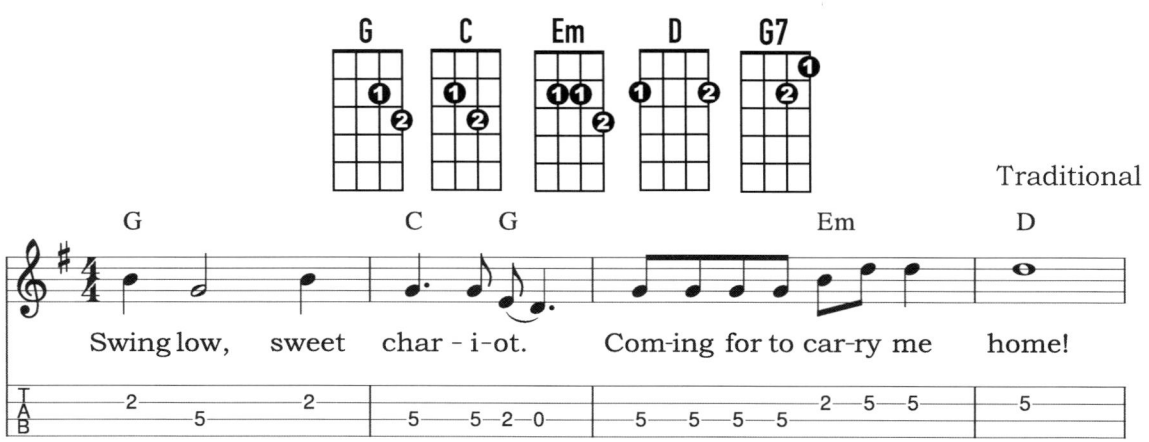

Traditional

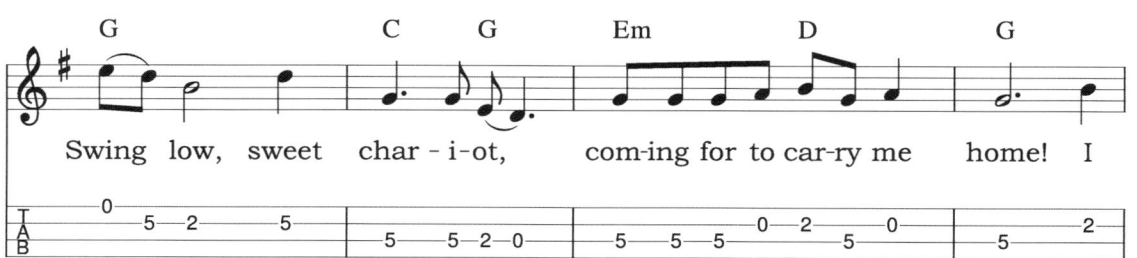

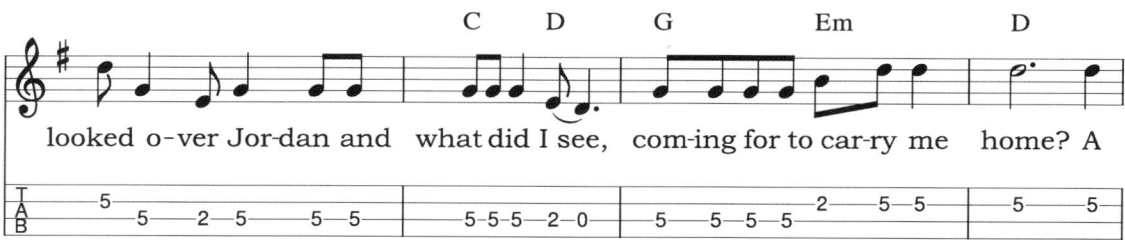

Swing low, sweet chariot,
Coming for to carry me home.
Swing low, sweet chariot,
Coming for to carry me home.

I looked over Jordan, and what did I see,
Coming for to carry me home.
A band of angels coming after me,
Coming for to carry me home. Oh,

Chorus

If you get there before I do,
Coming for to carry me home.
Tell all my friends I'm coming too,
Coming for to carry me home. Oh,

Chorus

The brightest day that ever I saw
Coming for to carry me home.
When Jesus washed my sins away,
Coming for to carry me home. Oh,

Chorus

I'm sometimes up and sometimes down,
Coming for to carry me home.
But still my soul feels heavenly bound,
Coming for to carry me home. Oh,

Chorus

Streets of Laredo

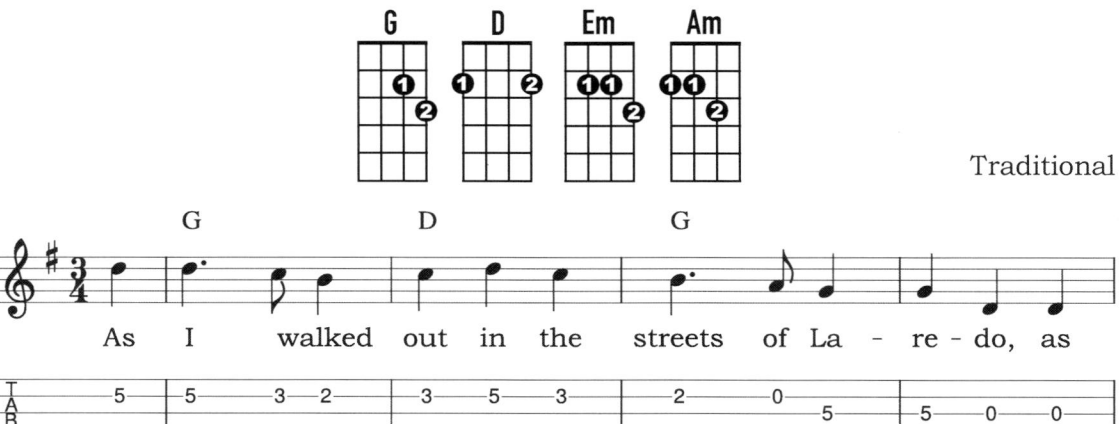

Traditional

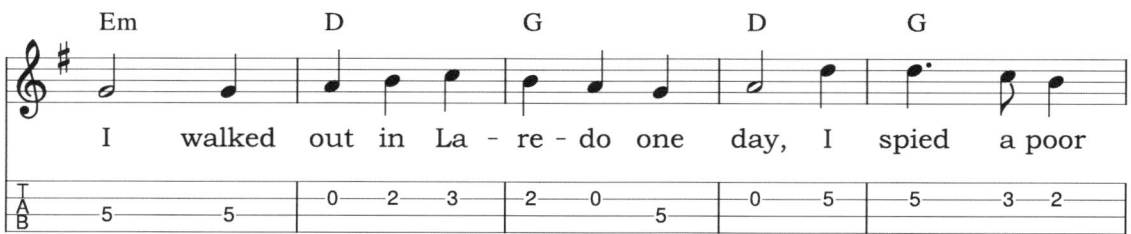

As I walked out in the streets of La - re - do, as

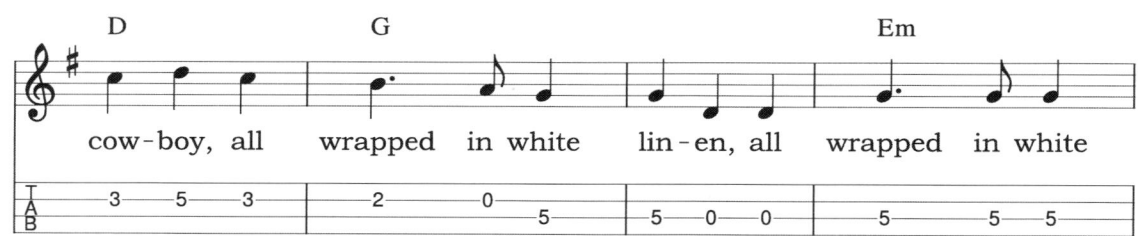

I walked out in La - re - do one day, I spied a poor

cow-boy, all wrapped in white lin-en, all wrapped in white

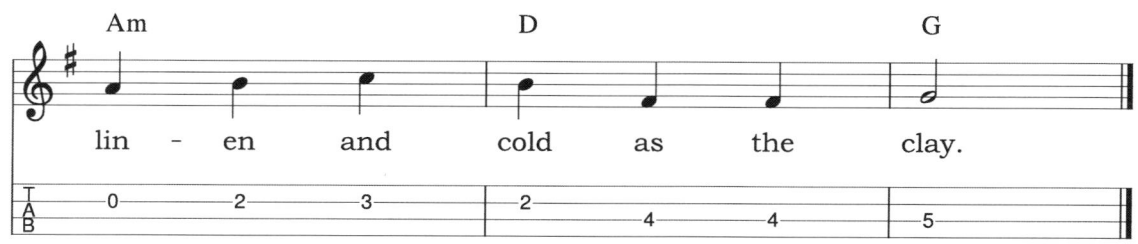

lin - en and cold as the clay.

As I walked out in the streets of Laredo
As I walked out in Laredo one day,
I spied a poor cowboy, all wrapped in white linen
All wrapped in white linen and cold as the clay.

"I see by your outfit, that you are a cowboy."
These words he did say as I slowly passed by.
"Come sit down beside me and hear my sad story,
For I'm shot in the chest, and today I must die."

"Oh once in the saddle I used to go dashing,
'Oh once in the saddle I used to go gay.
First down to Rosie's, and then to the card-house,
Got shot through the body, and now here I lay."

"Oh, beat the drum slowly and play the fife lowly,
And play the dead march as you carry me along;
Take me to the green valley, there lay the sod o'er me,
For I'm a young cowboy and I know I've done wrong."

"Get six jolly cowboys to carry my coffin,
Get six pretty maidens to bear up my pall.
Put bunches of roses all over my coffin,
Roses to deaden the clods as they fall."

"Then swing your rope slowly and rattle your spurs lowly,
And give a wild whoop as you carry me along;
And in the grave throw me and roll the sod o'er me.
For I'm a young cowboy and I know I've done wrong."

"Go bring me a cup, a cup of cold water.
To cool my parched lips", the cowboy then said.
Before I returned, his spirit had departed,
And gone to the round up – the cowboy was dead.

We beat the drum slowly and played the fife lowly,
And bitterly wept as we bore him along.
For we loved our comrade, so brave, young and handsome,
We all loved our comrade, although he'd done wrong.

Sweet Betsy from Pike

Traditional

Did you ever hear tell of Sweet Betsy from Pike,
Who crossed the wide mountains with her lover Ike,
And two yoke of cattle, a large yeller dog,
A tall Shanghai rooster, and a one-spotted hog.

Chorus:
Singing too-ra-li-oo-ra-li-oo-ra-li-ay.
Singing too-ra-li-oo-ra-li-oo-ra-li-ay.

They swam the wide rivers and crossed the tall peaks,
And camped on the prairie for weeks upon weeks.
Starvation and cholera, hard work and slaughter,
They reached California 'spite of hell and high water.

Chorus

One evening quite early they camped on the Platte,
'Twas near by the road on a green shady flat.
Betsy, sore-footed, lay down to repose
With wonder Ike gazed on that Pike County rose.

Chorus

Out on the prairie one bright starry night,
They broke out the whiskey and Betsy got tight.
She sang and she shouted and danced o'er the plain
And showed her bare arse to the whole wagon train.

Chorus

The Injuns came down in a thundering horde,
And Betsy was scared they would scalp her adored.
So under the wagon-bed Betsy did crawl
And she fought off the Injuns with musket and ball.

Chorus

The wagon broke down with a terrible crash,
And out on the prairie rolled all sorts of trash.
A few little baby-clothes, done up with care,
Looked rather suspicious, but all on the square.

Chorus

They stopped at Salt Lake to inquire of the way,
When Brigham declared that Sweet Betsy should stay.
Betsy got frightened and ran like a deer,
While Brigham stood pawing the ground like a steer.

Chorus

The alkali desert was burning and bare,
And Isaac's soul shrank from the death that lurked there.
"Dear old Pike County, I'll go back to you,"
Says Betsy, "You'll go by yourself if you do!"

Chorus

They soon reached the desert, where Betsy gave out,
And down in the sand she lay rolling about.
Ike in great wonder looked on in surprise,
Saying, "Betsy, get up, you'll get sand in your eyes."

Chorus

Sweet Betsy got up in a great deal of pain.
She declared she'd go back to Pike County again.
Ike gave a sigh, and they fondly embraced,
And they traveled along with his arm round her waist.

Chorus

The Shanghai ran off, and the cattle all died,
That morning the last piece of bacon was fried.
Ike got discouraged, Betsy got mad,
The dog drooped his tail and looked wonderfully sad.

Chorus

They suddenly stopped on a very high hill,
With wonder looked down upon old Placerville.
Ike said to Betsy, as he cast his eyes down,
"Sweet Betsy, my darling, we've got to Hangtown."

Chorus

Long Ike and Sweet Betsy attended a dance.
Ike wore a pair of his Pike County pants.
Betsy was covered with ribbons and rings.
Says Ike, "You're an angel, but where is your wings?"

Chorus

A miner said, "Betsy, will you dance with me?"
"I will that, old hoss, if you don't make too free.
Don't dance me hard, do you want to know why?
Doggone you, I'm chock-full of strong alkali."

Chorus

This Pike County couple got married, of course,
But Ike became jealous, and obtained a divorce.
Betsy, well-satisfied, said with a shout,
"Goodby, you big lummox, I'm glad you backed out!"

Sourwood Mountain

Bald Top Mountain

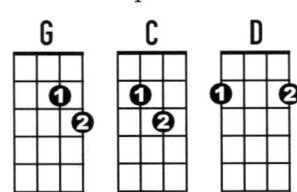

Traditional

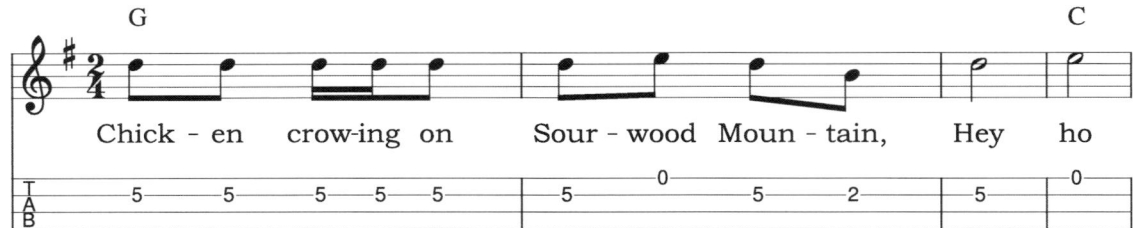

Chick - en crow-ing on Sour - wood Moun - tain, Hey ho

did-dle dum dee-ay, Get your dogs and we'll go a-hunt-ing.

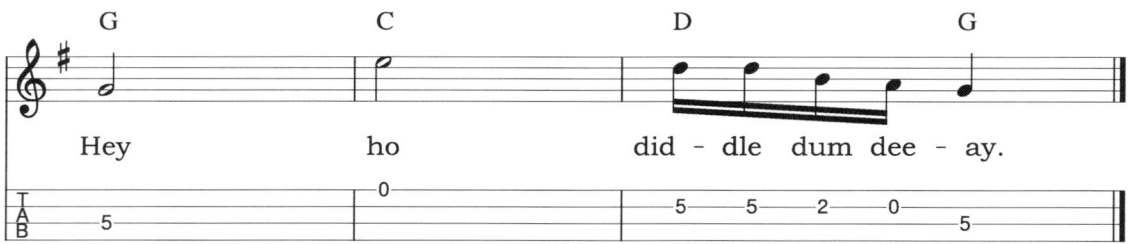

Hey ho did - dle dum dee - ay.

Chicken crowing on Sourwood Mountain,
Hey ho diddle dum dee-ay,
Get your dogs and we'll go a -hunting,
Hey ho diddle dum dee-ay.

Big dog bark and little one bite you,
Hey ho diddle dum dee-ay.
Big girl 'll court and little ono 'll slight you,
Hey ho diddle dum dee-ay.

My true love sho lives in Letcher,
Hey ho diddle dum dee-ay
She won't come and I won't fetch her,
Hey ho diddle dum dee-ay.

My true love lives up tho river,
Hey ho diddle dum dee-ay.
A few more jumps and I'll bo with her,
Hey ho diddle dum dee-ay.

My true love's a blue-eyed daisy,
Hey ho diddle dum dee-ay.
If I don't get her I'll go crazy,
Hey ho diddle dum dee-ay.

My true love livos in the hollow,
Hey ho diddle dum dee-ay.
Sho won't come and I won't follow,
Hey ho diddle dum dee-ay.

Tom Doolay

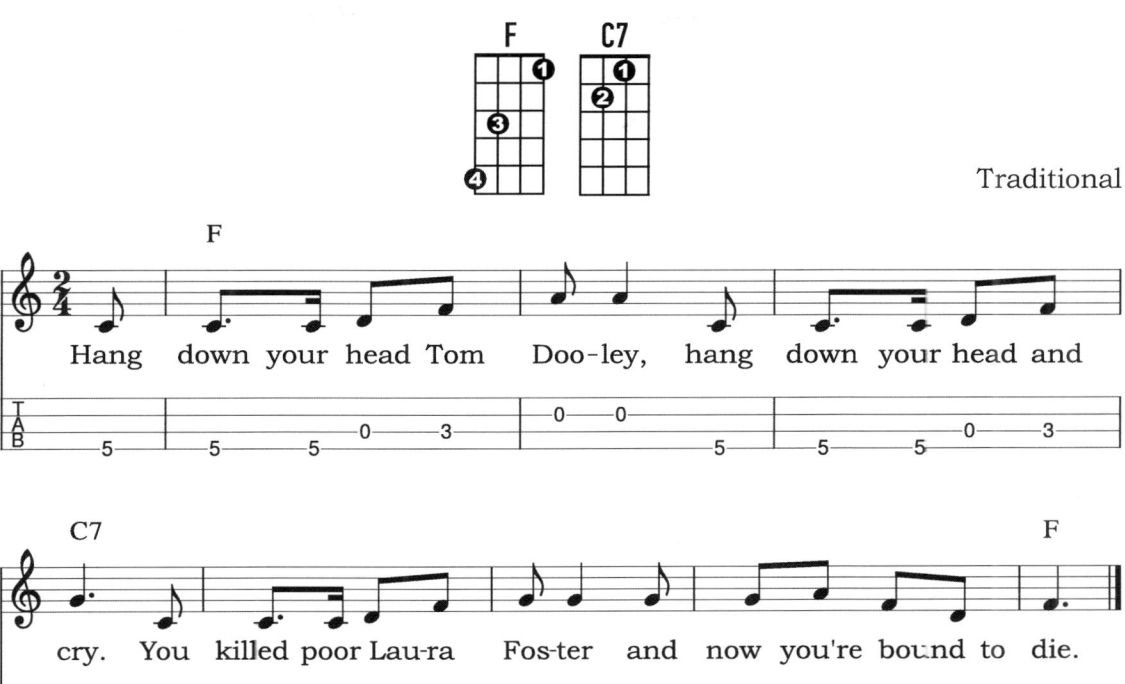

Traditional

Hang down your head Tom Doo-ley, hang down your head and cry. You killed poor Lau-ra Fos-ter and now you're bound to die.

Hang down your head Tom Dooley
Hang down your head and cry
Hang down your head Tom Dooley
Poor boy you're bound to die.

You met her on the hillside
And there you may suppose
You met her on the hillside
And there you hid her clothes.

Hang down your head Tom Dooley
Hang down your head and cry
Hang down your head Tom Dooley
Poor boy you're bound to die.

The Old Gray Mare

Traditional

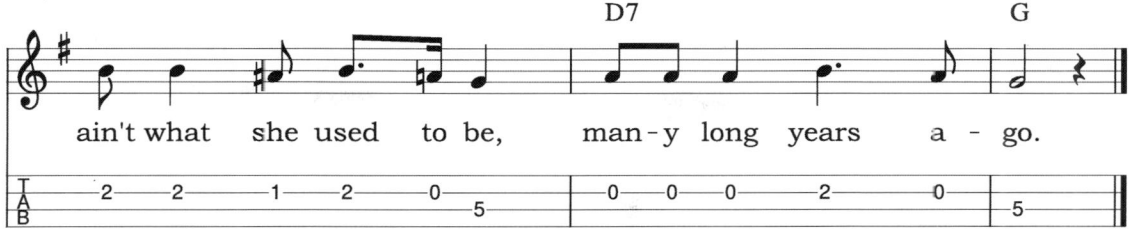

ain't what she used to be, man-y long years a - go.

The old gray mare, she ain't what she used to be,
Ain't what she used to be, ain't what she used to be,
The old gray mare, she ain't what she used to be,
Many long years ago.

Many long years ago, many long years ago,
The old gray mare, she ain't what she used to be,
Many long years ago.

The old gray mare, she kicked on the whiffletree,
Kicked on the whiffletree, kicked on the whiffletree,
The old gray mare, she kicked on the whiffletree,
Many long years ago.

Many long years ago, many long years ago,
The old gray mare, she kicked on the whiffletree,
Many long years ago.

75

Turkey in the Straw

Traditional

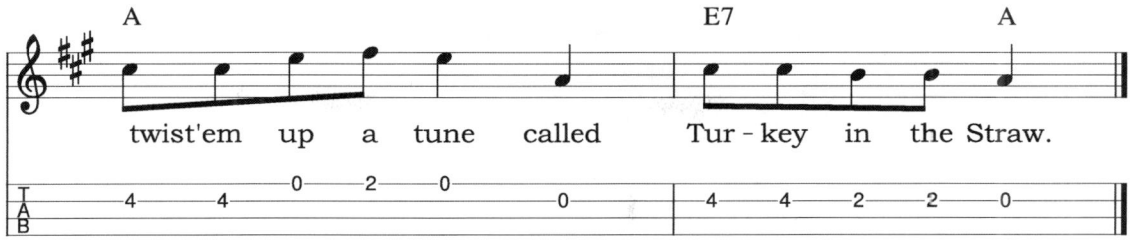

twist'em up a tune called Tur-key in the Straw.

As I was a-gwine down the road,
Tired team and a heavy load,
Crack my whip and the leader sprung,
l seys day-day to the wagon tongue.

Turkey in the straw, turkey in the hay,
Turkey in the straw, turkey in the hay
Roll 'em up and twist 'em up a high tuckahaw
And twist 'em up a tune called Turkey in the Straw.

Went out to milk, and I didn't know how,
I milked the goat instead of the cow.
A monkey sittin' on a pile of straw,
A-winkin' at his mother-in-law.

Met Mr. Catfish comin' down stream.
Says Mr. Catfish, "What does you mean?"
Caught Mr. Catfish by the snout,
And turned Mr. Catfish wrong side out.

Came to a river and I couldn't get across,
Paid five dollars for a blind old hoss;
Wouldn't go ahead, nor he wouldn't stand still,
So he went up and down like an old saw mill.

As I came down the new cut road,
Met Mr. Bullfrog, met Miss Toad
And every time Miss Toad would sing,
Old Bullfrog cut a pigeon wing.

Oh I jumped in the seat and I gave a little yell
The horses ran away, broke the wagon all to hell
Sugar in the gourd and honey in the horn
I never been so happy since the day I was born.

When the Boat Comes In

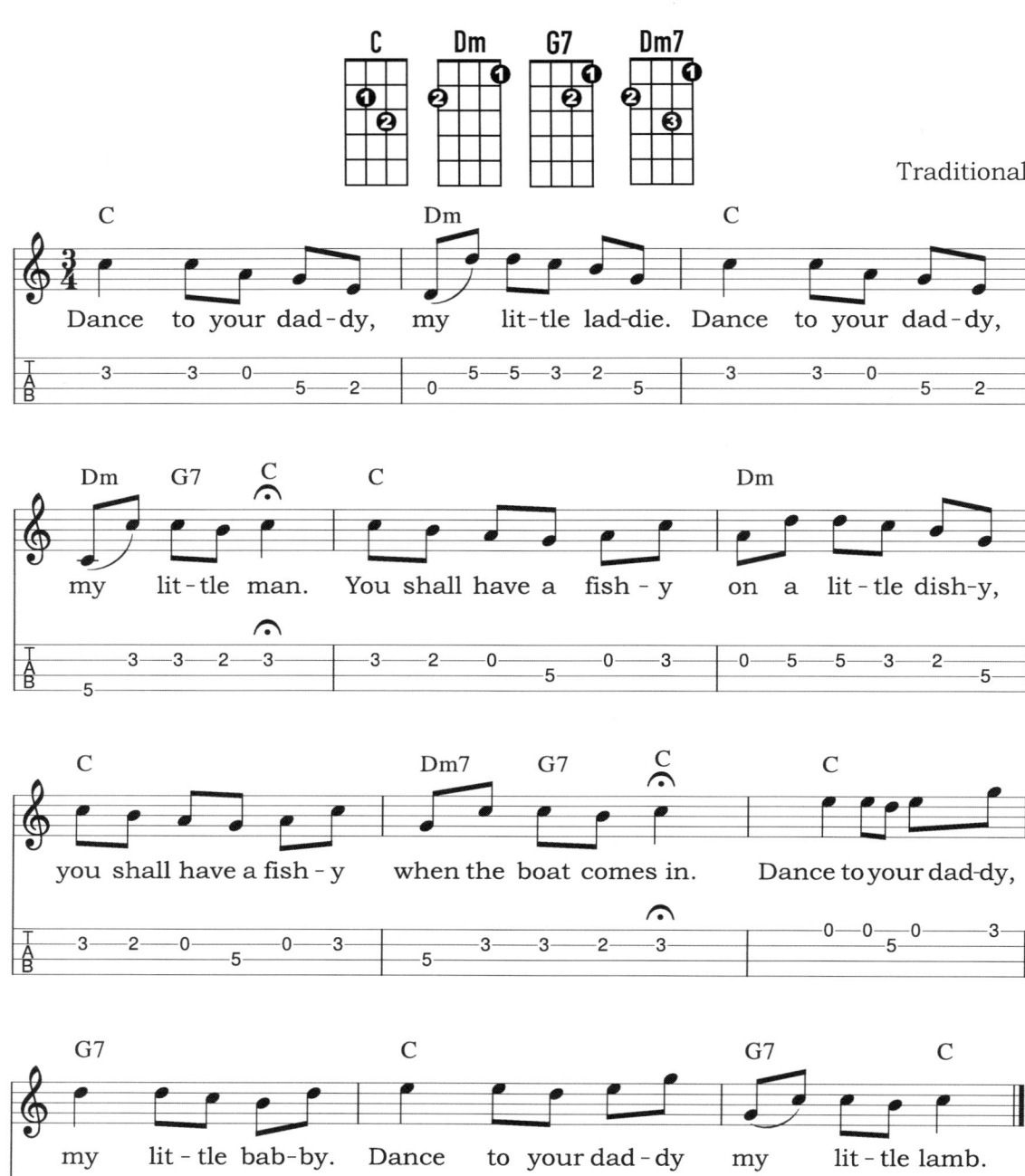

Traditional

When the Saints Go Marching In

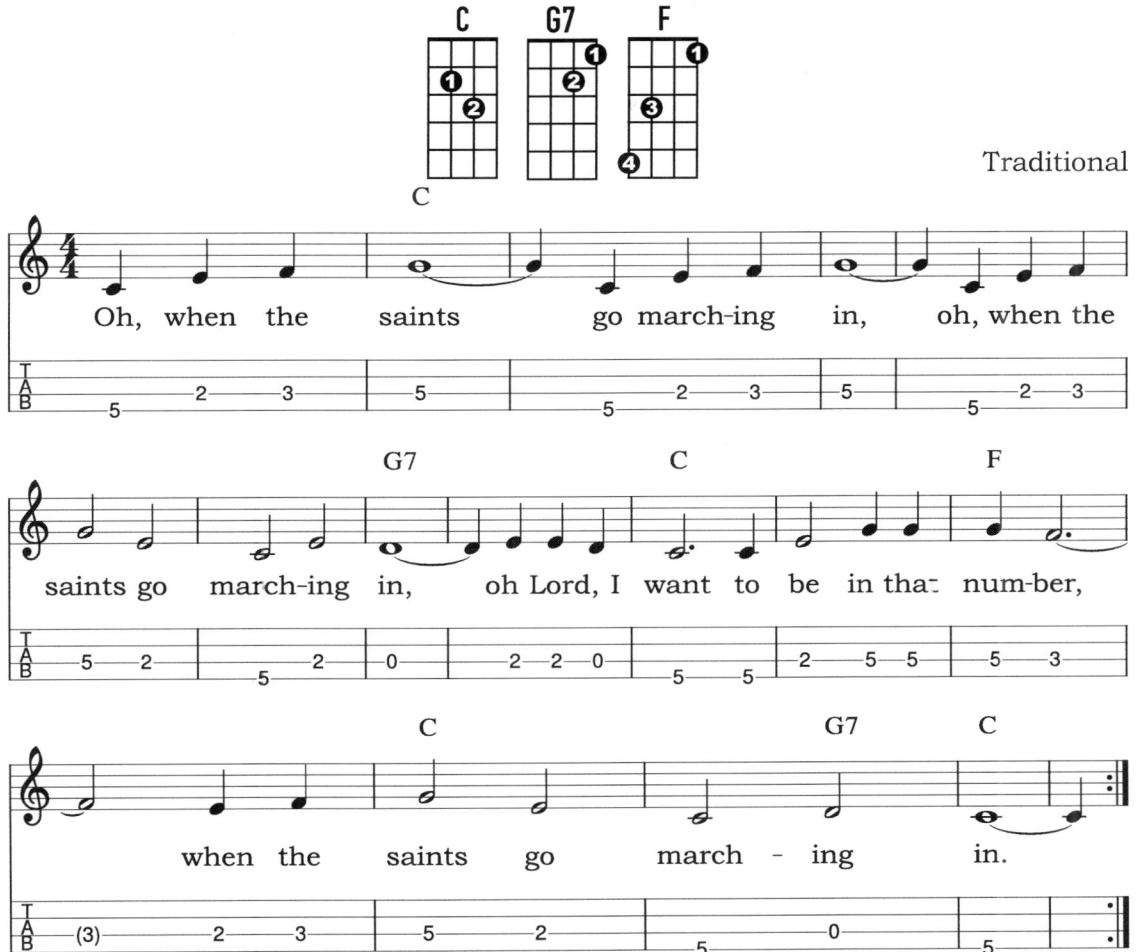

Traditional

Oh, when the saints go marching in, oh, when the saints go marching in, oh Lord, I want to be in that number, when the saints go march - ing in.

79

Oh, when the saints go marching in,
Oh, when the saints go marching in,
Oh Lord I want to be in that number,
When the saints go marching in.

Oh, when the drums begin to bang,
Oh, when the drums begin to bang,
Oh Lord I want to be in that number,
When the saints go marching in.

Oh, when the stars fall from the sky,
Oh, when the stars fall from the sky,
Oh Lord I want to be in that number,
When the saints go marching in.

Oh, when the moon turns red with blood,
Oh, when the moon turns red with blood,
Oh Lord I want to be in that number,
When the saints go marching in.

Oh, when the trumpet sounds its call,
Oh, when the trumpet sounds its call,
Oh Lord I want to be in that number,
When the saints go marching in.

Oh, when the horsemen begin to ride,
Oh, when the horsemen begin to ride,
Oh Lord I want to be in that number,
When the saints go marching in.

Oh, brother Charles you are my friend,
Oh, brother Charles you are my friend,
Yea, you gonna be in that number,
When the saints go marching in.

Oh, when the saints go marching in,
Oh, when the saints go marching in,
Oh Lord I want to be in that number,
When the saints go marching in.

Worried Man Blues

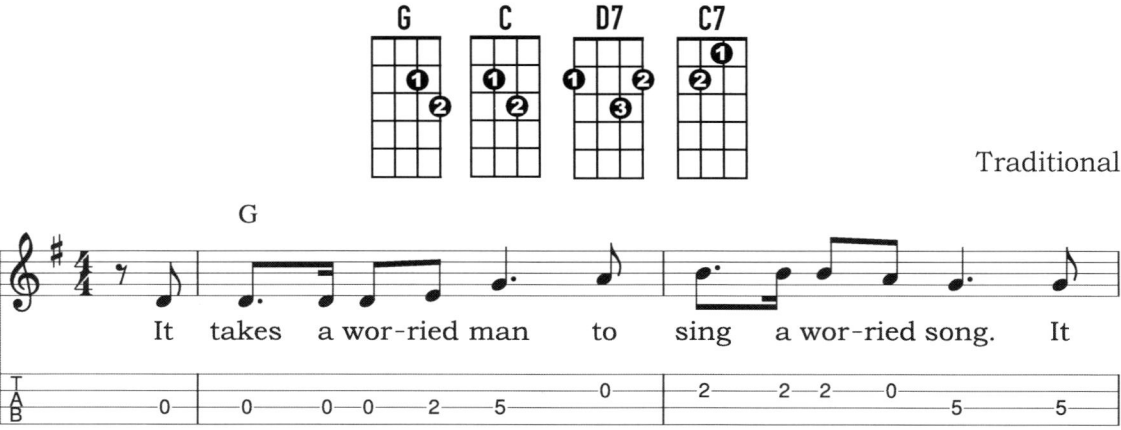

Traditional

It takes a worried man to sing a worried song.
It takes a worried man to sing a worried song.
It takes a worried man to sing a worried song.
I'm worried now, but I won't be worried long.

I went across the river and lay myself to sleep.
I went across the river and lay myself to sleep.
I went across the river and lay myself to sleep.
When I woke up, had shackles on my feet.

Twenty nine links of chain around my leg.
Twenty nine links of chain around my leg.
Twenty nine links of chain around my leg.
And on each link, an initial of my name.

I asked that judge, tell me, what's gonna be my fine.
I asked that judge, tell me, what's gonna be my fine.
I asked that judge, tell me, what's gonna be my fine.
Twenty-one years on that Rocky Mountain line.

Twenty-one years to pay my awful crime.
Twenty-one years to pay my awful crime.
Twenty-one years to pay my awful crime.
Twenty-one years, but I still got ninety-nine.

If anyone should ask you, who made up this song.
If anyone should ask you, who made up this song.
If anyone should ask you, who made up this song.
Tell 'em it was me, and I sing it all day long.

Yankee Doodle

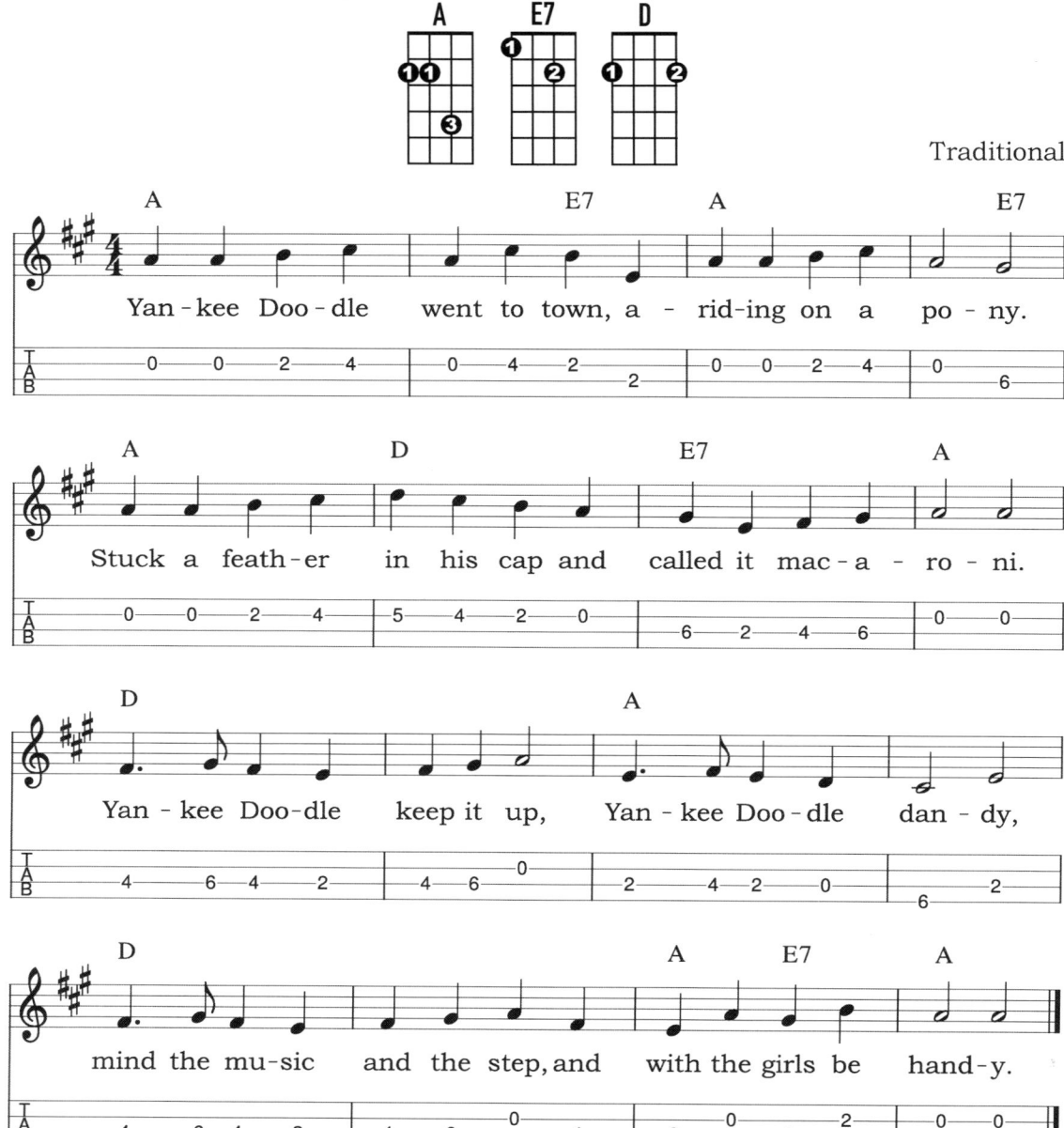

Traditional

Yankee Doodle went to town, a-riding on a pony.

Stuck a feather in his cap and called it macaroni.

Yankee Doodle keep it up, Yankee Doodle dandy,

mind the music and the step, and with the girls be handy.

82

Yankee Doodle went to town
A-riding on a pony,
Stuck a feather in his cap
And called it macaroni.

Yankee Doodle keep it up,
Yankee Doodle dandy,
Mind the music and the step,
And with the girls be handy.

Father and I went down to camp,
Along with Captain Gooding,
And there we saw the men and boys
As thick as hasty pudding.

Yankee Doodle keep it up,
Yankee Doodle dandy,
Mind the music and the step,
And with the girls be handy.

And there we saw a thousand men
As rich as Squire David,
And what they wasted every day,
I wish it could be savèd.

Chorus

The 'lasses they eat every day,
Would keep a house a winter;
They have so much, that I'll be bound,
They eat it when they've a mind to.

Chorus

And there I see a swamping gun
Large as a log of maple,
Upon a deuced little cart,
A load for father's cattle.

Chorus

And every time they shoot it off,
It takes a horn of powder,
And makes a noise like father's gun,
Only a nation louder.

Chorus

I went as nigh to one myself
As 'Siah's underpinning;
And father went as nigh again,
I thought the deuce was in him.

Chorus

Cousin Simon grew so bold,
I thought he would have cocked it;
It scared me so I shrinked it off
And hung by father's pocket.

Chorus

And Cap'n Davis had a gun,
He kind of clapt his hand on't
And stuck a crooked stabbing iron
Upon the little end on't

Chorus

And there I see a pumpkin shell
As big as mother's basin,
And every time they touched it off
They scampered like the nation.

Chorus

I see a little barrel too,
The heads were made of leather;
They knocked on it with little clubs
And called the folks together.

Chorus

And there was Cap'n Washington,
And gentle folks about him;
They say he's grown so 'tarnal proud
He will not ride without 'em.

Chorus

He got him on his meeting clothes,
Upon a slapping stallion;
He sat the world along in rows,
In hundreds and in millions.

Chorus

The flaming ribbons in his hat,
They looked so tearing fine, ah,
I wanted dreadfully to get
To give to my Jemima.

Chorus

I see another snarl of men
A-digging graves, they told me,
So 'tarnal long, so 'tarnal deep,
They 'tended they should hold me.

Chorus

It scared me so, I hooked it off,
Nor stopped, as I remember,
Nor turned about till I got home,
Locked up in mother's chamber.

Chorus

Made in the USA
Columbia, SC
28 January 2025

52900703R00048